Trust and Obey:

Man's Part in Joining
God's Family

KEN NISSEN

WESTBOW®
PRESS
A DIVISION OF THOMAS NELSON
& ZONDERVAN

Scriptures taken from the Holy Bible, New International Version®, NIV®.
Copyright © 1973, 1978, 1984, 2011 by Biblica, Inc.™ Used by permission
of Zondervan. All rights reserved worldwide. www.zondervan.com The "NIV"
and "New International Version" are trademarks registered in the United
States Patent and Trademark Office by Biblica, Inc.™ All rights reserved.

Scripture quotations taken from the New American Standard Bible®,
Copyright © 1960, 1962, 1963, 1968, 1971, 1972, 1973, 1975, 1977, 1995
by The Lockman Foundation. Used by permission." (www.Lockman.org)
The NASB is used unless otherwise noted. Scripture is given in italics.
Emphasis is by the author.

WestBow Press books may be ordered through booksellers or by contacting:

WestBow Press
A Division of Thomas Nelson & Zondervan
1663 Liberty Drive
Bloomington, IN 47403
www.westbowpress.com
1 (866) 928-1240

Because of the dynamic nature of the Internet, any web addresses or
links contained in this book may have changed since publication and
may no longer be valid. The views expressed in this work are solely those
of the author and do not necessarily reflect the views of the publisher,
and the publisher hereby disclaims any responsibility for them.

Any people depicted in stock imagery provided by Thinkstock are
models, and such images are being used for illustrative purposes only.
Certain stock imagery © Thinkstock.

ISBN: 978-1-4908-3475-7 (sc)
ISBN: 978-1-4908-3474-0 (e)

Library of Congress Control Number: 2014907134

Printed in the United States of America.

WestBow Press rev. date: 04/30/2014

Contents

Perhaps the main reason for the seeming contradiction between gift of salvation and the command to obedience Scriptures is a lack of proper understanding of "grace," "faith," and "works of the law," and we will try to deduce from Scripture the accurate meaning for each term as used in Scripture. And we will see how Paul fits the two sides together. Amazing!

Righteousness is the main theme in Romans: imputed righteousness and righteous living. In this study we will try to show that Paul's aim for Christians is what he calls "obedience of faith." Obedience of faith is our part by plugging into God's plan and grace. We shall see how righteousness comes by grace through faith, and is the opposite of "works of the law." How then does Paul's concept of the "obedience of faith" put the two together in Romans?

What does God really say about man's part in receiving His eternal life? Many Scripture verses on this topic are given here: (1) Those who are joined to Christ, (2) Those who are believing, (3) Those who believe with repentance, (4) Those who are born of the Spirit, (5) Those who believe with obedience, (6) Those who die to sin (7) Those who separate from the world, (8) Those who forgive others, (9) Those who surrender to God, (10) Those who fear God, (11) Those who do not fall away, (12) Those who remain faithful.

The Rev. Dr. Charles Stanley wrote a book entitled *Eternal Security, Can You Be Sure?* Dr. Stanley writes as though the Scriptures on man's part (obedience, faithfulness) do not count. At the end of each chapter he asks a question regarding man's part/God's part. In response to his position, I will seek to offer equally strong Scriptures that will demonstrate there is a beautiful balance in God's Word concerning God's part and man's part which Dr. Stanley seems to have missed/overlooked.

1 John was written that we may know that we have eternal life. How does he show us that? He gives us at least five authentic characteristics that show beyond any doubt that one is a child of God and destined for His eternal home.

In the next to the last chapter in the Bible God speaks and we learn what this whole creation story has been about. It also tells us in very clear words who will be there with Him and who will not.

For many years this writer lived under a false impression that he was secure for eternity. I was professing Jesus but living in fornication. God's Word says, *"I have forewarned you that those who practice such things shall not inherit the kingdom of God"* (Gal. 6:21). I learned I had to die to self. What does it mean to die to self?

KENNETH E. NISSEN BA in Biblical Education from Columbia Bible College; M Ed Masters in Education from University of South Carolina. He has been a teacher, counselor and administrator. He is married and has four children, nine grand children and one great-grandchild. Ken and his wife, Margaret, live in Irmo S.C. Ken has also written the book, *Revelation, God's Last Love Letter.*

Paradox

How can it be ???

There seems to be a contradiction in Scripture
on one of the most important questions:

What is man's part in receiving God's eternal life?

What does the Bible say?

ENDORSEMENT:

Dr. Robertson McQuilkin, President Emeritus of Columbia
International University, said concerning this essay:

*"...very good ... according to Scripture ... very
good ... I agree with everything in it ... I don't
think we will ever fully know God's part and
our part, but this is the closest I have ever seen
--- it is the best bridge I have seen ... I feel it is a
unique and much needed contribution. ..."*

There seems to be a contradiction in Scripture on one of the most basic of questions: what is man's part in receiving God's eternal life? Consider that each of the following verses is equally connected to eternal life:

Free gift: *"...but the free gift of God is eternal life in Christ Jesus our Lord"* (Rom. 6:23).

Yet obedience: *"...He became to all those who obey* [Gk. Present, are obeying] *Him the source of eternal salvation"* (Heb. 5:9).

By grace: *"For by grace you have been saved ..."* (Eph. 2:8).

Yet by deeds: *"And the world is passing away, and also its lusts; but the one who does the will of God abides forever"* (1 John 2:17).

By faith: *"For by grace you have been saved through faith* (Eph. 2:8).

And by perseverance: *"...by which also you are saved, if you hold fast the word which I preached to you, unless you believed in vain"* (1 Cor. 15:2—3).

Born again: *"...unless one is born again, he cannot see the kingdom of God"* (John 3:3).

And led by the Spirit: *"For all who are being led by the Spirit of God, these are sons of God"* (Rom. 8:14).

Righteousness reckoned: *"...God reckons righteousness apart from works..."* (Rom. 4:6).

Also righteousness by obedience: *"...you are slaves of the one whom you obey...of obedience resulting in righteousness"* (Rom. 6:16-17).

Not by works of the law: *"...nevertheless knowing that a man is not justified by the works of the Law but through faith..."* (Gal. 2:16).

Yet by good works: *"...for not the hearers of the Law are just before God, but the doers of the Law will be justified"* (Rom. 2:13). *"...who will render to every man according to his deeds: to those who by perseverance in doing good seek for glory and honor and immortality, eternal life"* (Rom. 2:6-7).

It is God working in you: *"...for it is God who is at work in you, both to will and to work for His good pleasure"* (Phil. 2:13).

But man is responsible: *"If anyone does not abide in Me, he is thrown away as a branch, and dries up; and they gather them, and cast them into the fire, and they are burned"* (John 15:6).

If eternal life is a "free gift" how can there be stipulations, conditions, or qualifications except to receive the free gift? In some Scripture it appears that God is responsible for all aspects of His salvation offered to men, but in others God seems equally to place responsibility on man to be obedient, to live righteously, and to be faithful to Him to the end. Some passages put the two elements side by side with both tied to eternal life:

But now having been freed from sin and enslaved to God, you derive your benefit, resulting in <u>*sanctification, and the outcome, eternal life*</u>*. 23 For the wages of sin is death, but the* <u>*free gift of God is eternal life*</u> *in Christ Jesus our Lord.* (Rom 6:2-23).

Here the gift of eternal life is to those who have become enslaved to God; obedient and holy, yet it is called a "gift." How can it be both by obedience and be a gift?

Many Evangelicals have long winked at this apparent contradiction, choosing to accept the *"free gift"* Scriptures as binding and spinning the "obedience" Scriptures in many various ways to a non-mandatory status. In this study we will try to show that in Romans Paul calls *"obedience of faith"* the purpose of his ministry, and that the correct understanding of this term resolves the problem by embracing both elements in harmony. If this study fails to clarify the apparent contradiction, then there must be some other explanation, but the issue is too important to ignore.

We feel that the answer to this question is important because the belief system that one holds determines how he lives. If one believes the teaching that man needs to merit righteousness,[1] that one is likely to depend on self-effort and self-merit to be saved. If one believes that righteous living is not essential, that one is likely to compromise with the world, the flesh and the devil. Both legalism and licentiousness are erroneous with disastrous ends. There could be multitudes with false assurance of eternal life. Maybe the answer is what Paul calls *"obedience of faith"* (Rom. 1:5).

Perhaps the main reason for the seeming contradiction between free gift and obedience is a lack of proper understanding of "grace," "faith" and "works of the law," and we will try to deduce the accurate meaning from Scripture for each term.

GRACE

When I was in high school a pastor said, "Mercy is befriending someone who is in trouble, but grace is befriending someone who has been your enemy." And I observed others using grace as a mercy, so for many years I believed "grace" was a type of mercy. And another definition that is often given, "unmerited favor," is similar in definition to that of mercy. Of course anything God gives us short of hell is from His mercy (or unmerited favor), but that does not properly

---

[1] Note that our English words "justify" and "righteous" come basically from the same Greek root word "dikaios" having to do with being legally innocent and morally upright. Also the English word for "believe" (verb) and "faith" (noun) come from the same basic Greek root word "pisteuo" (verb) and "pistis" (noun).

portray the meaning of grace as used in the New Testament when God is the source. The Greek word "charis" originally meant "favor, gift, or thanks," and that is how the New Testament uses "charis" when it is grace expressed from man to another man.

When "charis" is expressed from man to God it always means "thanks." That is why we say "grace" at mealtime. Sometimes when reading the New Testament one could use "unmerited favor" as a substitute for grace, but the meaning for grace when it comes from God is God's "provision" or "enabling." When God's provision or enabling is substituted for "charis" it fits perfectly and makes the passage meaningful. Here are example verses that show "<u>grace</u>" from our loving, merciful, gracious God as His "provision/enabling":

> And now I commend you to God and to the word of His <u>grace</u> (provision), which is able to build you up and to give you the inheritance among all those who are sanctified (Acts 20:32).
>
> For if by the transgression of the one the many died, much more did the grace (provision) of God and the gift by the grace (provision) of the one Man, Jesus Christ, abound to the many (Romans 5:15).
>
> And God is able to make all <u>grace</u> (provision) abound to you, that always having all sufficiency in everything, you may have an abundance for every good deed (2 Corinthians 9:8).
>
> And He has said to me, "My <u>grace</u> (enabling) is sufficient for you, for power is perfected in weakness." Most gladly, therefore, I will rather boast about my weaknesses, that the power of Christ may dwell in me (2 Corinthians 12:9).
>
> And I thank Christ Jesus our Lord who has <u>enabled</u> (graced) me, because He counted me faithful, putting me into the ministry (1Timothy 1:12 NKJV).

I thank Christ Jesus our Lord, who has strengthened
(graced) me, because He considered me faithful, putting
me into service (1 Tim 1:12 NAS).
I thank Christ Jesus our Lord, who has given
me strength (grace), that he considered me faithful,
appointing me to his service (1 Tim 1:12 NIV).

That grace is God's provision is emphasized in Ephesians 2:8-9: *"For by grace* (God's provision) *you have been saved through faith; and that not of yourselves* (your provision), *it is the gift of God* (God's provision); *not as a result of works* (your provision), *that no one should boast."* So we may seek to be saved of ourselves/our works or as God's gift by grace (God's provision). God's provision is contrasted with our provision. God said one must be trusting in His provisions, not in one's own works/provisions.

That grace is God's "provision" rather than His "mercy" (or unmerited favor) makes a huge difference. The basis of God's grace is the Son's atonement for cleansing from the penalty of our sin, and the indwelling of the Holy Spirit that we may live free from the captivation of sin. Because of the provision and enabling of the indwelling Spirit we have the opportunity to respond to God and partake of His great salvation.

We are able to repent, we are able to commit, and we are able to obey; all because of His grace. God has provided the way and means for us to be holy and live in His holy presence. He amply provides the provision and enabling, but we are responsible for appropriating it through faith. The net result: He holds us responsible for repenting, faith, love and obedience. If we falter and sin it will be due to our lack of appropriating His grace — not His lack of provision/enabling.

In Romans 4:16 Paul explains why faith and grace go together as God's way of salvation, *"For this reason it is by faith, that it might be in accordance with grace, in order that the promise may be certain to all the descendants, not only to those who are of the Law, but also to those who are of the faith of Abraham.*" The only way that "*it*" (God's salvation) can be certain is if it depends upon God and His provision. If any part of it depended upon my plan, my provision, or my good works it could not be "*certain*," but it is by His plan, His provision and His enabling, thus it can be "*certain*" to all who partake "*by faith.*" But what is "faith"? *Faith* is depending upon God by actively participating in His grace (His provision).

FAITH

Salvation comes "*by faith*" or "*through faith.*" For years I wondered why "**faith**" was so magical that it could open the gates to eternity — it seemed to resemble Aladdin when he would say, "Open sesame." And a study of "*by faith*" and "*through faith*" in the Epistles reveals a power far beyond that of Aladdin.

1. Faith Works

In Scripture when man expresses meaningful "faith" to God it is not just mental agreement, it is an active, productive, working relationship. **"The Hebrews regarded faith as something that one does rather than as something one has. It is an activity rather than a possession."²**

In 1 Thessalonians we read, "*constantly bearing in mind your <u>work of faith</u>*" (1 Thess.1:3; also 2 Thess.1:11; Jam.2:26). It is important to see that faith works. Faith that is Biblical faith produces something, it works. So, whether it is justification, establishing the law, or performing acts of righteousness, it works. It is not that the person has power or authority, but because he is calling on the promises and power (provision/enablement) of God. Since God will always

---

² Erickson, Millard J. *Christian Theology.* (Grand Rapids: Baker Book House, 1989), p.938.

support what He has promised, one can make it applicable to himself by appropriating the promise. God invites us to freely partake of all His vast provisions/supply (grace), and He will even enable (grace) us to do this. No wonder it is more powerful than Aladdin. We draw on the resources of the Almighty.

Faith is man connecting to God as a branch to the vine or as a refrigerator into the electric power circuit. The power of God is such that it can transform a once sinful, unregenerate man to one who produces obedient behavior/good deeds — by faith.

Therefore *"by faith"* (acting with dependence upon God for His effort and supply) is the opposite of legalism (acting with dependence on self-initiated effort to be spiritually beneficial and productive). So faith is an activity of man, but it is linking up with and utilizing the power and provision of Almighty God. Notice some of the ways in Scripture that **faith works**: *"...justified by faith, righteousness which is by faith, walk by faith, live by faith, united by faith, lived as an alien, received ability to conceive, were not afraid of the king's edict, kept the Passover, the walls of Jericho fell down, did not perish, conquered kingdoms, performed acts of righteousness, obtained promises, shut the mouths of lions..."*

2. Faith Perseveres

Faith does have a beginning, an initial life, but like a newborn baby it grows. It grows in trust and obedience unto the end. Paul's emphasis on faith is reiterated often in Romans, as in 1:16 and 17. The gospel of God is for everyone – everyone, that is, who *"believes"* [Greek present, is believing]. He states, *"the righteousness of God is from faith to faith"* — not just initial *"faith,"* but from faith to faith to faith — all the way. Quoting from the Old Testament he said, *"the righteous man shall live by faith."* The way of salvation is a life-long attitude of faith. It is faith that last to the end:

And because lawlessness is increased, most people's love will grow cold. But the one <u>who endures to the end, he shall be saved</u> (Mat.24:12-13).

By which also <u>you are saved, if you hold fast the word</u> which I preached to you, <u>unless you believed in vain</u> (1 Cor.15:2).

Maybe one reason Christians misunderstand "believe" today is because of the way our Bible translators have translated the Greek verb *"pisteuo"* into the English counterpart. The Greek language made clear whether the action of the verb was considered having been done at a point in time or whether it was continuous and on-going action/activity. It is very unfortunate that our English translations do not give this distinction (even though they could), so that our translations that now read *"whoever believes"* (or believeth) does not inform us of the original intent. Actually on the occasions when "believe" is used regarding an individual's salvation the present or continuous mode, "is believing," is used with all but rare exceptions. Here are a few examples:

But as many as received Him, to them He gave the right to become children of God, even to those who believe [Gk. present, is believing] in His name (John 1:12).

For God so loved the world, that he gave his only begotten Son, that whoever believeth [Gk. present, is believing] in him should not perish, but have everlasting life (John 3:16).

Even the righteousness of God through faith in Jesus Christ for all those who believe [Gk. present, are believing]; for there is no distinction … (Rom. 3:22).

But to the one who does not work, but believes [Gk. present, is believing] in Him who justifies the ungodly, his faith is reckoned as righteousness (Rom. 4:5).

For with the heart man believes [Gk. present, is believing], resulting in righteousness, and with the mouth he confesses, resulting in salvation (Rom. 10:10).

It is important to understand that "believe" is an action verb [faith is the noun], and that it is continuing action for salvation. God gives the grace to believe and He gives the grace to continue to believe, there is no difference; that is, initial believing is of His provision by faith and continuing to believe is of His provision by faith. All is the gift of God.

3. Faith Is Connecting/Joining/Abiding

"For this reason it is by faith, that it might be in accordance with grace, in order that the promise may be certain to all the descendants" (Rom.4:16). So why is it "faith" that makes it possible for us to live "by grace"? Faith is like a branch abiding in the vine or like a refrigerator plugged into the electric current to receive the life/power to function. So faith is connecting to God for fellowship, guidance, and strength (for His provision - grace).

All of God's provisions (grace) are available by plugging into Him as a branch into the vine or a refrigerator into the electric power line. *"Abide in Me, and I in you. As the branch cannot bear fruit of itself, unless it abides in the vine, so neither can you, unless you abide in Me* (John 15:4). Just as the electric appliance (or branch) can only work as it is plugged into the power source, Jesus said we can only work for God as we are plugged into Him.

When we plug in our electric appliances we pay the electric company for the use of that power, right? When we plug into Jesus, how much does He charge? He says His power (grace) is His free gift to us — no payment, no works on our part. That is how God's salvation is said to be His free gift to us in Christ Jesus. Eternal life and all of His gifts are ours as we are "**in Christ**": *"Praise be to the God and Father of our Lord*

Jesus Christ, who has blessed us in the heavenly realms with <u>*every spiritual blessing*</u> ***in Christ*** (Eph 1:3 NIV). Thank you Lord Jesus!!!

In the passage on the Vine and the branches, who is commanded to make and keep the connection? We are. God is the source of the fruit, but who is responsible if there is no fruit? We are. God provides (grace), and we are responsible for tapping into Him (faith).

It is important to note that one cannot be abiding into two or more basic allegiances at one time. In order to *"abide"* or to "plug into" Christ, one must first "unplug" from himself (dependency on his own wisdom, effort, and schemes for earning any goodness or spiritual merit with God). So then, faith is choosing to "unplug" from my provision and myself and to "plug" into Jesus, to depend on Him for His provision/ enabling/power (grace).

We *"grow in grace"* (2 Pet.3:18) when we trust and obey Him. He is then able to reveal to us more of what we need to commit to Him.

Works of the Law

Paul said we are not under law but under grace (Rom. 6:14-15). We are dead to the law, and *"We have believed in Christ Jesus, that we may be justified by faith in Christ, and* <u>*not by the works of the Law*</u>*; since by the works of the Law shall no flesh be justified"* (Gal. 2:16). Jesus confronted the problem of *"works of the law"* with the Pharisees. The Judaizers and Pharisees thought they were acceptable to God by who they were and/or what they did to merit acceptance. Today we call this legalism. This tendency of self-merit is the natural tendency of the human heart, and we see it in every religion. It creeps into Christianity in various obvious and insidious forms.

It is easy to spot in something like burning candles for the dead. But reliance on church affiliation, Bible study, tithing, and such may also actually be a form of works, and it may be granting a false sense of security. Some may trust in these works while continuing to participate in pornography, lust, dishonesty, gossip, anger and such, and believe that they will be excused. But not according to what Paul told the church: *"...carousing, and things like these, of which I forewarn you just as I have forewarned you that those who practice such things shall not inherit the kingdom of God"* (Gal. 5:21).

But what about the law? Is mandatory obedience legalism? We would refer you to the fine section on Law and Grace in Robertson McQuilkin's book, *An Introduction to Biblical Ethics*[3] for a more detailed study in this area, but for this paper we will quote some excerpts from this chapter.

"Ceremonial and national elements of the law, along with some moral laws, are clearly set aside. Indeed, the entire dispensation seems to have been disallowed by Paul as having binding authority on Christian conscience. But the Ten Commandments and moral law as law are constantly reaffirmed. On this basis we apply Old Testament teaching to Christian life and doctrine.

The law is good (Rom.7:12), the law is spiritual (v.14), the law is continuing in effect (Matt.5:17-19), but it is only good if it is used lawfully, as it was intended (1Tim.1:8).

In the Bible freedom is not license to do what we please, but power to do what we ought. And what we ought is to obey the will of God.

Having to do something is not legalism (1Tim. 3:2; Eph.5:28; 2 Thess.1:3; Rom.15:27)...Having a list of

---

[3] McQuilkin, Robertson; *An Introduction to Biblical Ethics.* (Wheaton: Tyndale House Publishers, 1989) pp.45-82

don'ts is not legalism (Rom.12:2; Col. 3:9; Gal.6:9; Eph.4:25—5:18; 1 John 2:13)...It is not legitimate to call a society "legalistic" simply because it has many laws. If so, the Bible is indeed one of the most legalistic of all books.

Thus law and grace are two sides of the single coin of God's salvation. Without grace, law is a terrifying destroyer. Without law, grace is meaningless. Each is true only as the other is rightly understood. As Jesus said, those who set aside the least of God's laws will indeed be least in his realm (Matt. 5:18-19).

Must I do it? Yes. Must I do it whether I want to or not? Yes. Must I do it no matter what my motivation? Yes. That is what law means. Of course, if love sets the spirit free, God's commandments are no longer a grief (1 John 5:3). Then I will long to obey this law as my high privilege."

God's law, God's nature, God's character has never changed. Sin is missing the mark of God's law. The only way for us to know what is right, just, and loving is to obey what He says. As McQuilkin pointed out, the moral issue with Adam and Eve was obedience. All of God's heavenly beings obey the Almighty. Obedience has not been supplanted. But grace (God's provision) has been added in a new way that we may be able to obey, and Christ's love has been demonstrated so that obedience is our great joy and privilege. Jesus said, *"If you love me you will keep my commandments"* (John 14:15). Paul said it is *"faith working through love"* (Rom.5:6). Through faith we may live a life of love and obedience by the provision of God.

The question is asked in Romans 6:15, *"Shall we sin because we are not under law but under grace?"* Paul then answers that question: *"...you are slaves of the one whom you obey, either of <u>sin resulting in death</u>, or of **<u>obedience resulting in righteousness</u>**?"* So death is the result of sin, and righteousness and eternal life is the result of obedience. He repeats this in verse 22: *"But now having been freed from sin and **enslaved to God**, you derive your benefit, resulting in sanctification, and **the outcome, eternal life**."*

Eternal life is the result of obedience/sanctification! Then he summarizes in verse 23, *"**For** the wages of sin is death, but the free gift of God is eternal life in Christ Jesus our Lord."* Notice that verse 23 begins with *"for"* (or because) indicating the *"free gift"* of verse 23 relates back obedience/sanctification result in eternal life of verse 22. So, just as the eternal life is a gift from God, obedience and sanctification are likewise the gift of God, the fruit of the Holy Spirit. It is critical to see this.

Obedience of Faith

God made man in His own image to commune with Him as a friend, a companion, a child, even a bride. The point of the story of mankind is God bearing children for His eternal home (Rev. 21:1-8). God's question to man is, "Who wants Me, who will choose Me?" The question is not who acknowledges there is a God, not even who acknowledges Jesus died for his sins; but who chooses to join Him, His kingdom, and His ways. He is love, He is holy, and He is Lord.

Those who join Him must reject the sinful, selfish ways of the world and choose His ways. Those who join Him must join Him as the Lord that He is — or they do not really join Him at all: *"For whoever wishes to save his life shall lose it; but whoever loses his life for My sake and the gospel's shall save it. For what does it profit a man to gain the whole world, and forfeit his soul"* (Mark 8:35-36)?

But His ways are beyond our reach. Who can be holy? Who can love in an unselfish way? Who can forgive a major hurt? We are not capable. God must enable us, provide inside help, and He does. This "enabling," this "inside help" of His Holy Spirit is called His <u>grace</u>. And how do we secure this provision of God for ourselves? <u>By faith</u>. Faith is like the branch drawing on the vine, or the power cord drawing on the power line — which connects us to God.

Yet it is not tangible, not visible, not a thing, but a choosing — choosing to reject my way in exchange for God, His desires, and His way. It is choosing to accept God's promise of eternal life regardless of the cost in this life. Faith, in essence, is our joining to God, and this, God said, is what He desires. When we disconnect from ourselves and connect to God He can do great spiritual things in us and through us.

If one has chosen God as his god, his life will demonstrate it. He will begin to think and act more and more as God does. The key characteristic of that person is obedience of faith. Jesus said, *"And why do you call Me, 'Lord, Lord,' and do not <u>do</u> what I say"* (Luke 6:46)? Obedience is so clearly aligned with love and faith that God said it is the basis of His judgment of who will have eternal life with Him:

> *"Who will render to every man <u>according to his deeds</u>: to those who by perseverance in <u>doing good</u> seek for glory and honor and immortality, <u>eternal life</u>; but to those who are selfishly ambitious and do not <u>obey</u> the truth, but <u>obey</u> unrighteousness, <u>wrath</u> and indignation"* (Rom. 2:6-8).

Is God's gift of His Son free to those who believe in Him? Yes. Our faith response and the repentance and the openness it produces are both enabled by God's grace. Is the grace of God that enables us to live righteously the free gift of God also? Yes. Our "good works" in this case are the fruit of the Holy Spirit; all of God and in no way contributes to any self-merit on our part. Does God hold us responsible for turning away from sin and unto His holiness (sanctification)? Yes. We must continue to choose between obeying our fleshly desires or obeying Him. Does God hold us responsible for maintaining our allegiance to Him? Yes. The one thing we can give Him is the one thing He desires — our love and loyalty (and He even provides the enabling for us to do that).

Is God's salvation a free gift by grace through faith alone? Yes. Are Scriptures that tie repentance, obedience, love, and sanctification to eternal life just as binding and mandatory as the free gift verses? Yes. How can it be? Because grace is God's provision/enabling, and faith is our plugging into Him for His grace. It is all by His grace — but I am responsible for plugging into Him for this grace.

"So then, my beloved, just as you have always <u>obeyed</u>... work out your salvation with fear and trembling; for it is God who is at <u>work in you</u>, both <u>to will</u> and <u>to work</u> for His good pleasure" (Phil. 2:12-13). It is God who works in us to will and to do of His good pleasure — all of God, all free. But, God holds us responsible for obeying by "plugging into" Him (faith) so that we can receive His provision (grace). This is what Paul calls *"obedience of faith."* Paul said this was the goal of his ministry. Should it not be our goal also?

> *"We have received grace and apostleship to bring about the <u>obedience of faith</u> among all the Gentiles, for His name's sake."* (Rom. 1:5)

"Obedience of Faith"

in

ROMANS

"Reckoned as righteousness" (4:5)

And

"Obedience resulting in righteousness" (6:16)

PREFACE

Through the many centuries since the apostle Paul there have been many theories and a sharp divide regarding the teaching of justification/righteousness as it relates to man's part in God's salvation. The theme of Romans is righteousness for it is the condition needed by sinful man to be right with God (1:17). There are verses that state that justification/ righteousness is reckoned to man as God's gift on the basis of Christ's atonement: *"Being justified as a gift by His grace through the redemption which is in Christ Jesus"* (3:24), and there are verses that state that man's effort is also necessary in the realization of God's salvation *"You are slaves of the one whom you obey, either of sin resulting in death, or of obedience resulting in righteousness"* (6:16).

In my previous essay entitled "Paradox," I quoted numerous verses that illustrate eternal life from both the "free gift by grace through faith" verses, and from obedience/sanctification verses. In that study we tried to show how verses concerning eternal life from obedience/sanctification are equally by God's grace (His provision) through our faith (plugging into God's grace). For since our obedience is by the power of the Spirit, it is just as much the gift of God as our initial believing, and is considered by Paul likewise to be the gift of God. Paul calls this *"obedience of faith"* and this bridges the gap between God's provision and our desperate need of righteousness.

Righteousness is the main theme in Romans — imputed righteousness and righteous living. In this current study we will try to show that Paul's aim for Christians is what he calls *"obedience of faith."* Obedience of faith is our part by plugging into God's plan and provision (grace). We shall see how righteousness comes by grace through faith, and is the opposite of *"works of the law."* How then does Paul's concept of the *"obedience of faith"* emerge and develop in his epistle to the Romans? Let us begin the first portion of chapter one, in which Paul presents the purpose of the entire epistle.

CHAPTER 1:1–17. The Purpose of Romans

In verse one Paul states three things about himself – he is a slave, he is an apostle, and he is set apart for the gospel. He had been born free, but of his own free will, he had chosen to be a slave. In our human societies a slave is the lowest rank, but in God's kingdom to be God's servant/slave is our greatest honor. With a great price we were purchased from the pits of hell, and obedience to Christ is our great joy. A servant is one who obeys. Jesus said, *"Why do you call me Lord, Lord, and not do what I tell you?"* (Luke 6:49). The obedience of Christ is our model, *"Have this attitude in yourselves which was also in Christ Jesus ...He humbled Himself by becoming obedient to the point of death, even death on a cross"* (Phil 2:5-8).

In chapter one, verse five, Paul states the purpose of the grace and apostleship given to him – *"to bring about the obedience of faith..."* [Some translations misrepresent the Greek text by using "obedience of <u>the</u> faith"] When I first saw this I was surprised to learn his purpose was obedience. Obedience is not a noble goal in our modern democratic society. Paul's goal, however, was not for more obedience "per se"; it was for a special kind of obedience: *"of faith"* obedience. Paul will repeat this goal two more times at the end of Romans (15:18; 16:26).

In Scripture when man expresses meaningful "faith" to God it is not just mental agreement, it is an active, productive, working relationship. **"The Hebrews regarded faith as something that one does rather than as something one has. It is an activity rather than a possession."[4]** Paul agreed and said, *"works of faith"* (or faith works. 1Thess.1:3). Faith "works": *"justified by faith, righteousness which is by faith, walk by faith, live by faith, united by faith."* Faith is man

---

[4] Millard J. Erickson *CHRISTIAN THEOLOGY.* Baker Book House. 1989 p.938.

connecting to God as a branch to the vine or a refrigerator into the electric power receptacle. The power of God is such that it can transform a once sinful, unregenerate man to one who produces good deeds by faith.

Paul's emphasis on faith is reiterated in verse 16 and 17. The salvation of God is for everyone – everyone, that is, who "*believes*" [Greek present tense, is believing]. He states, "*The righteousness of God is from faith to faith*" – not just initial "*faith*," but **from** faith **to** faith **to** faith…all the way. Quoting from the Old Testament he said because, "*The righteous man shall live by faith.*" The way of salvation is a life of faith.

CHAPTER 1:18–32. Wrath Against Disobedience

The latter part of chapter one speaks of the grievous evil of mankind. Man is aware of God's eternal power and divine nature yet he suppresses the truth in unrighteousness. Therefore God will be just in judging all unrighteousness in His day of wrath. Paul describes in detail the unrighteous nature of man — the reason for God's coming wrath.

CHAPTER 2:1–29. Judgment According to Deeds

The first part of chapter two speaks to those who agree that those "other people" are evil and deserve death, but do not include themselves (as the Jews did). Paul reminds them that those who sit in judgment of others are also guilty of the same sins, and God's wrath will be revealed against all unrighteousness. In the first chapters of Romans Paul is showing the desperate need the sinful world has for the righteousness of God, because the wrath of God is coming against all disobedience: "*But to those who are selfishly ambitious and do not obey the truth, but obey unrighteousness, wrath and indignation. There will be tribulation and distress for every soul of man who does evil, of the Jew first and also of the Greek"* (2:8-9).

In the next segment Paul speaks of the necessity of righteous living/obedience. This passage states clearly that eternal life will be for those who persevere in good deeds: "To *those who by perseverance in doing good seek for glory and honor and immortality, eternal life"* (2:7). This sounds like salvation by works. This seems to contradict many other passages: (1) that say no one has done good deeds, (2) that salvation is a gift for those who are in Christ, not those doing good, and (3) that *"works of the Law"* are actually contrary to God's way.

Because of this apparent contradiction there have been numerous theories of what other possibilities this passage in Romans 2 may mean besides what it actually says. But the passage must either be taken as a concrete assertion or an abstract hypothesis. Except for the notion that it seems to conflict with other Scripture, there is no other reason to suppose it does not actually mean what it says.

Suppose Paul meant what he said; does it "fit"? Paul's purpose is *"obedience of faith,"* and in this passage he speaks of *"those who are selfishly ambitious and do not <u>obey</u> the truth, but <u>obey</u> unrighteousness, <u>wrath</u> and indignation"* (2:8). These are contrasted *"to those who by perseverance in <u>doing good</u> - <u>eternal life</u>"* (2:7). Back and forth he states that those who do not do good or do not obey will receive wrath, but to those who do good — they will *"receive glory and honor and peace,"* whether Jew or Gentile (2:10) because *"the doers of the law will be justified"* (2:13).

The criterion by which judgment is to be executed *"according to his deeds"* is not different than other Scriptures found elsewhere. For example,

> "... [they] *shall come forth; <u>those who did the good deeds</u> to a resurrection of life, those who committed the evil deeds to a resurrection of judgment"* (John 5:29).

"And these will go away into eternal punishment, but the righteous into eternal life" (Matt.25:46).

"Not everyone who says to Me, 'Lord, Lord,' will enter the kingdom of heaven; but he who does the will of My Father who is in heaven" (Matt. 7:21).

"When the righteous turns from his righteousness and commits iniquity, then he shall die in it, But when the wicked turns from his wickedness and practices justice and righteousness, he will live by them" (Ezek.33:18-19).

"And having been made perfect, He became to all those who obey Him the source of eternal salvation" (Heb.5:9).

Therefore, one should accept what God has given in the text. The apparent contradiction is clarified later in chapter 8.

Chapter two concludes with the conviction that what is important with God is not whether a person is a Jew, but whether one is circumcised of the heart by the Spirit, *"But he is a Jew who is one inwardly; and circumcision is that which is of the heart, by the Spirit"* (2:29). God hates outward sham, but He loves submission from the heart.

CHAPTER 3:1–20. The Jews and "Works of the Law"

In the first half of chapter three Paul answers a series of questions that a Jew should ask to prevent false assurance. He has a common answer to his questions: God is righteous, and He will judge in righteousness. The Jews had the advantage of receiving the Word of God, but, *"It [the Law] speaks to those who are under the Law, that every mouth may be closed, and all the world may become accountable to God"* (3:19). The Jews had the Law, but their deeds were evil for selfish purposes. Both Jew and Gentile alike are permeated with evil. Having the Law only reveals the sin more and is not a way to justification.

Paul closes this section concluding that all are sinful/ unrighteous and not holy for God's holy kingdom. He further concludes that *"works of the law"* (or trying to be righteous by keeping the law) is untenable. Paul uses *"works of the Law"* as the opposite of *"obedience of faith"/"good works."* So, those who figure that by who they are and/or what they do will grant them entrance to God are mistaken because all of us are evil.

CHAPTER 3:21–31. Justification Comes Through Christ by Faith

In verse 28 Paul sets forth that God's way of righteousness is by faith: *"But now apart from the Law the righteousness of God has been manifested, being witnessed by the Law and the Prophets, even the righteousness of God through faith in Jesus Christ for all those who believe"*(3:21).

Paul presents this as the gift of God by grace, *"Being justified as a gift by His grace through the redemption which is in Christ Jesus"* (3:24). God's grace (provision) for our justification is the atonement for our sins: *"as a propitiation in His blood through faith"* (3:25). And it is through "faith" (plugging into God's provision).

Paul then goes on the offensive: justification by faith does not negate the Law – it actually establishes it: *"Do we then nullify the Law through faith? May it never be! On the contrary, we establish the Law"* (3:31). How does faith establish the Law? His answer will come in chapter eight.

CHAPTER 4. Righteousness has always been Reckoned by Faith

But first Paul uses two Old Testament figures to say that God's way of righteousness has always been by faith. Three times in chapter four Paul quotes from the Old Testament that faith *"was reckoned to him as righteousness."* It was *"reckoned"* (counted, imputed) because of faith. Paul said righteousness in the Old Testament was by way of faith, and it still is God's only way to righteousness. God reckoned righteousness to Abraham based on what Christ would do, and it is based for us on what Christ did do – the same sacrifice, no difference in that the faith is in God. God has said that His provision is sufficient, and we are to believe Him. Eleven times the term "reckoned" is used in chapter four. Because of Christ's atonement God may reckon sins as forgiven to those who are believing (plugging into/joined to Him).

In 4:16 Paul explains why faith and grace go together as God's way of salvation, *"For this reason it is by faith, that it might be in accordance with grace, in order that the promise may be certain to all the descendants, not only to those who are of the Law, but also to those who are of the faith of Abraham."* The only way that *"it"* (God's salvation) can be certain is if it depends upon God and His provision, and the only way to connect to God is by faith. If any part of it depended upon my plan, my provision, or my good works it could not be *"certain."*

Notice from verse 16 onward that Abraham's faith was working. It was working against all odds, even when there seemed to be no way God's promise could come true for both he and Sarah were *"good as dead"* as far as having children. But, *"Being fully assured that what He had promised, He was able also to perform. Therefore also it was reckoned to him as righteousness"* (4:21).

Faith was working to continue to give him full hope and assurance. Therefore it was reckoned to him as righteousness.

CHAPTER 5. The Grace of God in Christ is His Unmerited Gift

In this chapter Paul states that we are *"justified by faith"* (5:2). In verse nine he states we are *"justified by His blood."* The atonement of Jesus is the basis or grounds for God to forgive our sin, and faith is the means by which we tie into His provision (grace) for forgiveness.

Paul eloquently describes the love and grace (provision) of God toward us who are still in disobedience and under His pending wrath. He emphasizes that all of God's goodness and grace come to us by way of His dear Son.

Paul contrasts how everyone is affected by the two "Adams": all in Adam are under a curse of death, and all in Christ are under God's gift of life. In contrast to the way in which death reigned from Adam,*" Those who receive the abundance of grace and of the gift of righteousness will reign in life through the One, Jesus Christ"* (5:17). He continues, *"As through one man's disobedience the many were made sinners, even so through the obedience of the One the many will be made righteous"* (5:19).

As sin produced death, grace (God's provision) produces righteousness and life (vs.21). Many Evangelical leaders confine the *"made righteous"* to imputed righteousness only, or to a future eternal state. But the contrast Paul gives here can only match a life of righteousness in our present bodies: that as we formerly lived as disobedient people from Adam's fall, we now live obediently through Christ Jesus, the second Adam.

CHAPTER 6. Joined to Sin or to Christ

In this chapter Paul asks two questions about grace. Actually it is one question with two answers. The question is whether we may continue in sin since we are under grace?

First: *"Are we to continue in sin that grace might increase?"* He answers immediately: *"May it never be! How shall we who died to sin still live in it?"* (6:1-2). One who joins Christ is one who has likewise totally rejected sin. Otherwise he has not joined to the holy God.

So Paul asks how can it be that one who has chosen to reject sin for a new life with Christ (pictured in baptism) — how can that one continue to obey sin? He said, *"May it never be."* Notice that as God *"reckoned"* Christ's atonement for the penalty of our sins, we are to *"reckon"* ourselves to be dead to sin but alive unto God (vs.11).

Paul's second part is similar: *"Shall we sin because we are not under law but under grace?"* Again Paul answers immediately: *"May it never be! Do you not know that when you present yourselves to someone as slaves for obedience, you are slaves of the one whom you obey, either of sin resulting in death, or of obedience resulting in righteousness?"* (6:15-16).

Paul makes a clear black and white: everyone is a slave (obedient) to sin or to righteousness. He states in no ambivalent words that anyone who is living as a slave to sin will receive death, and the ones obedient to God are the righteous. He repeats this and summarizes in vs. 22: *"But now having been freed from sin and enslaved to God, you derive your benefit, resulting in sanctification, and the outcome, eternal life."* So the answer to whether we should continue in sin since we are under grace: not if we want eternal life!

Paul has been speaking much about faith before this chapter — believing into Jesus. In chapter six Paul gives a clear understanding of what "believing into" means to him. To believe into Jesus means total commitment, total identification, and total allegiance as symbolized by baptism. Lest anyone should maintain false hope that partial surrender or occasional allegiance is acceptable, Paul states there are only two alternatives: slavery to sin (the end is death) or slavery to righteousness (the end is eternal life). If one is a slave he has a master/owner. So, we are either owned by self (and whatever gods and life style we may choose) or, if we are slaves of righteousness, we are owned by God.

Notice carefully that verse 22 states that obedience leads to righteousness and to eternal life, yet verse 23 says, *"But the free gift of God is eternal life in Christ Jesus our Lord."* How can eternal life be by obedience (vs.22), but it is a free gift (vs.23)? Because obedience of faith is plugging into God's grace (provision); so that our obedience is by God's power, His gift by His Spirit.

In this chapter Paul asked shall we continue in sin? The answer is "no" because we gave up sin to live with Christ when we joined Him (symbolized by baptism); and "no" because if we continue in sin the wages of sin will be death. But if we are slaves to righteousness, God's gift is eternal life.

CHAPTER 7. Death to Self Effort

Chapter seven is dealing with the question relating back to verse 6:15 regarding being under grace now rather than under law. Paul here states that we died to the old rituals and ceremonies of the law when we joined Christ, and we now serve in newness of the Spirit that we may bear fruit unto God.

In verse seven Paul asks a new question: *"Is the Law sin?"* Again Paul answers promptly saying, *"May it never be! On the contrary, I would not have come to know sin except through the Law."* He continues and he demonstrates that the problem is not the Law, rather it is our sinful nature: *"Wretched man that I am! Who will set me free from the body of this death? (7:24).*

CHAPTER 8. There is Therefore Now no Condemnation

In chapter 8 we receive the solution we need to the problem! Chapters 1-3 showed our sinfulness and need of righteousness. Chapters 4 and 5 revealed God's provision in Christ through faith for forgiveness. Chapters 6-7 declared the need to continue in righteousness even though we are now under grace. Then the end of chapter 7 demonstrates our need of power for righteousness in our lives. So we have a big problem: *"Who will set me free from the body of this death?"* Paul's quick answer: *Thanks be to God through Jesus Christ our Lord!* (7:24-25). It is through Jesus Christ. But how does Christ help me live in righteousness? That leads to chapter 8.

At the opening of this chapter we are informed that all who are now in Christ Jesus are not under condemnation, *"There is therefore now no condemnation for those who are in Christ Jesus* (Rom.8:1). Paul gives the answer why, *"For the law of the Spirit of life in Christ Jesus has set you free from the law of sin and death"* (8:2). In other words we are no longer under condemnation because we are no longer tied to the law of self-effort for righteousness (next verse) — Jesus has condemned sin: *"For what the Law could not do, weak as it was through the flesh, God did: sending His own Son in the likeness of sinful flesh and as an offering for sin, He condemned sin in the flesh"* (Rom 8:3).

But what about the requirement of keeping the Law/living righteously? We are no longer under condemnation there either because the Son has made provision (grace) for us that we shall keep the Law; next verse: *"...in order that the requirements of the Law might be fulfilled in us"* (8:4). The requirements are going to be fulfilled in us? [Notice it does not say imputed to us] Now we are back to 3:31, *"we establish the Law"* and we live in righteousness.

We have tried and we always fail, how are we going to live righteously? Next Paul gives the answer, *"For if you are living according to the flesh, you must die; but if by the Spirit you are putting to death the deeds of the body, you will live. For all who are being led by the Spirit of God, these are sons of God"* (8:13-14).

So, if by the Spirit we are putting to death the deeds of the body, and if the Spirit is leading us, we are then establishing the Law; that is, we are fulfilling the requirements of the law and living righteously. Therefore, it is not we who do it, but the Spirit of God working in us and through us.

That is why Paul said, *"There is therefore now no condemnation"* — not only are our sins covered by the atonement, but we put to death the evil deeds and live in righteousness by the Spirit. The Spirit leads us. The only way to find our way through the maze of worldliness is to follow the Spirit. How do we follow the Spirit? We follow the Spirit by learning what God has said in His Word and obeying it. The Spirit enables (grace) us to learn His Word and to obey it.

So, in chapter eight we now see God's power for *"obedience of faith"* and for *"perseverance in doing good,"* which leads to *"eternal life"* (2:7). It is by exercising faith (connecting to His provisions), to obey the Word of God, by the enabling of the Spirit of God.

Faith in God "works." Who does the "works," God or man? There is Scripture that says it is all of God and to His glory, and Scripture that places the responsibility on man and gives reward to man. So it is a joint activity from a relationship. As Paul said, *"It is no longer I who live, but Christ lives in me"* (Gal 2:20); and *"My grace* [provision] *is sufficient for you... that the power of Christ may dwell in me"* (2 Cor.12:9-10). Is it all of God? Yes. Have we any merit for boasting? No. Is man's participation in his righteousness required? Yes.

Now we can see the whole picture of God's way to transform sinful man into righteous man fit for His holy family. Is it all of God's provision (grace) in Jesus? OH YES! Is it any of man's self-effort to bargain with God? On the contrary it is by faith — by connecting to God, His plan, His provision, His power. Does man have a vital part? YES. It is the work of faith: faith that chooses God, faith that submits to God, faith that trusts God regardless of the temptations to desert Him, faith that

rejoices in the great assurance of His impending return —
faith that works.

In the latter part of chapter 7 we saw constant struggle
and defeat. After we learn God's provision by His Spirit we
find the opposite — victory: *"For you have not received a
spirit of slavery leading to fear again, but you have received a
spirit of adoption as sons... heirs of God and fellow heirs with
Christ...that we may also be glorified with Him."* (8:15-17).
Wow! What a glorious, merciful gift God gives to those who
put to death the deeds of the body and follow the Spirit. The
remainder of the chapter eight exalts in this new position and
the security it provides — all by the power of God. And we tie
into it by FAITH.

CHAPTERS 9–11. Israel's Disobedience and Gentiles' Obedience

In Romans 3:3 Paul asked the question, *"What then? If some
did not believe, their unbelief will not nullify the faithfulness
of God, will it?"* In chapters nine to eleven he answers that
question. Israel did not arrive at righteousness because they
did not pursue it by faith (9:32-33). Gentiles who pursue it by
faith do attain to it (9:30).

In chapter ten Paul said Israel sought righteousness
on their own (10:3), *"They did not subject themselves to the
righteousness of God."* Then Paul repeats that Christ is the
end [Greek "telos": aim, purpose, finish] of the Law (10:4), and
Paul expounds on the message of faith, *"for with the heart man
believes* [Greek present tense, continually believes] *resulting
in righteousness, and with the mouth he confesses, resulting
in salvation"* (10:10).

In chapter eleven Israel is seen as a branch broken off and
Gentiles grafted into its place. Israel was broken off because
of their unbelief/disobedience (11:20, 23, 30, 31), and Gentiles
now stand by faith, only if they remain in faith: *"Quite right,*

they were broken off for their unbelief, but you stand by your faith" (11:20). So he instructs, *"Do not be conceited, but fear; for if God did not spare the natural branches, neither will He spare you"* (11:21).

Israel believed they were immune from the judgment of God because they were His chosen ones rather than because they were His righteous ones by faith. Paul is saying here to the church that we are likewise immune from God's wrath only as we are righteous by faith. We are to be obedient, not unbelieving. We are to be righteous people, made so by the enabling power of the Holy Spirit at work in us. This is not optional for those who are part of the kingdom of the holy God.

CHAPTERS 12 – 16. Therefore Present Yourself

In 12:1 there is a big "***therefore***."

"***Therefore***" because I want to glorify the great God of all wisdom and knowledge (previous paragraph),

"***Therefore***" because I know the wrath of God is upon the ungodliness of sinful man (1:18),

"***Therefore***" because God will judge men according to their deeds (2:6),

"***Therefore***" because the wages of sin is death (6:23),

"***Therefore***" because self-effort is self-defeating (7:24),

"***Therefore***" because God in His love and grace (provision) has demonstrated unimaginable sacrifice to win my love and devotion (5:8),

"***Therefore***" because in Christ I may have life eternal (5:10),

"***Therefore***" because I may become part of God's family (8:15),

> *"**Therefore**"* because the end will turn out the way He
> said it would (8:39),
> *"**Therefore**"* because God's way is the way of faith
> (4:16),
> *"**Therefore**"* ***present your bodies as a living
> sacrifice....*"**

There are many *"mercies of God"* reasons why we should *"therefore... present your* [our] *bodies a living and holy sacrifice"* (all on the altar, total surrender of self-will). The only question that really matters in life is: **"Is Jesus Lord"**? To have a Master is to be in subjection – to obey. We are to obey when we feel like it, and we are to obey when we don't. We are to obey when there is something we like to do, and we are to obey when we don't want to.

We are to concur with Paul that, *"For me to live is Christ."* Jesus gave the same message, *"If anyone wishes to come after Me, let him deny himself, and take up his cross, and follow Me. For whoever wishes to save his life shall lose it; but whoever loses his life for My sake and the gospel's shall save it"* (Mark 8:34-35).

Since faith is connecting to God like the branch to the vine or the refrigerator into the power line, it makes sense that one cannot be connected to two different sources. We are either plugged into ourselves or we are abiding in Christ. Step one in faith is to present ourselves as living sacrifices for Christ – we cease from plugging into ourselves, and we plug into Christ. This is our *"holy sacrifice,"* our *"spiritual service of worship"* — our great privilege.

If step one in the life of faith is surrender of one's self, step two is from verse two, *"be transformed* [present tense, be being transformed] *by the renewing of your mind"* (12:2). Paul has already alluded to this in 8:6: *"For the mind set on the flesh is death, but the mind set on the Spirit is life and peace, because the mind set on the flesh is hostile toward God; for it does not subject itself to the law of God, for it is not even able to do so."*

The mind, affections, and will (sometimes referred to as the "heart" or "inner man") must be given over to being renewed, re-taught, retrained, and even *"transformed."* The emphasis here, as in much of Scripture, is on the *"mind."* The mind is the rudder of the soul, so it must be kept on a straight course. It is essential that one's mind be "set" upon God in order to be trained to think as God thinks. It is from the mind-set that attitudes are formed and grow. Jesus said that heaven would be composed of those who had begun developing attitudes such as *"poor in spirit," "peace maker," "pure in heart," "hunger and thirst after righteousness,"* and *"forgiveness"* (Matt.5:3, 9; 6:14).

Step three in the life of faith is righteous living in the chaotic, selfish, deceitful world of everyday life. The remainder of Romans deals with this aspect of righteousness. Paul has already touched on this aspect also: *"For all who are being led by the Spirit of God, these are sons of God"* (8:14). The only way to find our way through the maze of worldliness is to follow the Spirit. How do we do this? We follow the Spirit by learning what God has said in His Word and obeying it. We are informed about how to live with our brothers, our neighbors, and our leaders. His commands are summed up in *"love"* — *"Love does no wrong to a neighbor; love therefore is the fulfillment of the law"* (13:10).

And if we fulfill the Law we *"establish the Law"* (3:31). This is the way of *"obedience of faith."* In chapter 15 Paul again states his goal, *"For I will not presume to speak of anything except what Christ has accomplished through me, resulting in the **obedience of the Gentiles** by word and deed"* (15:18). And again in the conclusion in chapter 16, *"Now to Him who is able to establish you ... leading to **obedience of faith**; to the only wise God, through Jesus Christ, be the glory forever. Amen"* (16:25-27).

CONCLUSION

Many groups of people, such as the Pharisees, Roman Catholics, and Modernists to name a few, have put a spin on the Word of God to their detriment and harm to the Kingdom. Today, Evangelicals claim to be the keepers of the Word of God. Yet when God clearly and repeatedly says that obedience and righteous living are not optional, where are "the keepers"? Are there multitudes today with false security because of "the keepers"?

Israel had the problem of believing that they were immune to God's wrath because they were chosen people. Paul did not want any false security so he made it clear that ALL who are living according to the flesh must die, *"for if you are living according to the flesh, you must die"* (8:13). He said to the Galatians' church: *"Now the deeds of the flesh are evident, which are: immorality, impurity, sensuality, idolatry, sorcery, enmities, strife, jealousy, outbursts of anger, disputes, dissensions, factions, envying, drunkenness, carousing, and things like these, of which I forewarn you just as I have forewarned you that those who practice such things <u>shall not inherit the kingdom of God</u>* (Gal 5:19-21).

The key difference between the kingdom of God and the kingdom of this world is "righteousness." Romans, as well as the rest of Scripture, deals with the need for righteous living. Unfortunately there are some today, like Israel of old, who read the Word of God and feel they are excused from it. God's message is righteousness reckoned to us (4:5), AND sanctification (a life of righteousness) (6:1-22).

Thankfully the message of salvation apart from our schemes and our effort is made abundantly clear today in Evangelical circles. We praise God that salvation is in Christ Jesus and His work alone, for we have no merit to offer. Man is sinful and spiritually bankrupted. He never has anything to offer to God as merit or leverage to bargain with God and any attempt to do so is self-effort (legalism), which is an affront to

God and contradicts and negates God's provision (grace). This part is made clear. But can we choose which part of God's Word we will believe and which we will ignore or spin?

Grace (God's provision) is what we need; it is all we need. It provides for initial cleansing, imputed righteousness, continual cleansing, and righteous living. It provides for initial relationship with Jesus Christ and continual relationship with Him. God's grace is given to enable us to continually be in right relationship to the holy God. So God's grace enables us to *"walk in the light as He is in the light"* (1 John 1:7). Obedience and righteous living are not optional, *"...anyone who does not practice righteousness is not of God"* (1 John 3:10). The purpose of grace and God's aim for us is, *"to become conformed to the image of His Son"* (Rom 8:29). We are created, *"for good works, which God prepared beforehand, that we should walk in them"* (Eph 2:10).

God's grace is available to all men, but it is effectual only for those who plug into it (faith). One must forsake self-effort for self-gain (legalism) and embrace God's grace (provision) by faith. Faith is man connecting to the grace of God by calling on Him and counting on Him to keep His promises. And the needed obedience and righteous living come only from His grace (enabling) by faith (connecting to His provision) — the product of the indwelling Spirit of God.

One is either a slave to self and sin, or a slave to God (Rom.6:16-18). According to God there are no other options. Obedience of faith is the only cure for unrighteousness. And only the righteous are part of God's holy kingdom (6:22).

The Gift Of Salvation
By Grace Is For

(NASB – Not in italics – Emphasis by K.E.N.)

1. Those who are Joined to Christ:

John 1:12 But as many as <u>received Him</u> [aorist, point action], to them He gave the right to become children of God, {even} to those who believe [present tense, are believing] in His name.

Eph. 1:7-9 In Him we have redemption through His blood, the forgiveness of our trespasses, according to the riches of His grace, which He lavished upon us...according to His kind intention which He purposed in Him.

Col. 1:19-20 For it was the {Father's} good pleasure for all the fullness to dwell in Him, and through Him to reconcile all things to Himself, having made peace through the blood of His cross; through Him, {I say} whether things on earth or things in heaven.

Rom. 3:24 ...being justified as a gift by His grace through the redemption which is in Christ Jesus.

Rom. 6:23 ...but the free gift of God is eternal life in Christ Jesus our Lord.

Rom. 8:1 There is therefore now no condemnation for those who are in Christ Jesus.

1 Cor. 1:30 But by His doing you are in Christ Jesus, who became to us wisdom from God, and righteousness and sanctification, and redemption.

1 Cor. 15:22...for as in Adam all die, so also in Christ all shall be made alive.

2 Tim. 1:9...who has saved us, and called us with a holy calling, not according to our works, but according to His own purpose and grace which was granted us in Christ Jesus from all eternity.

1 John 5:11-13...And the witness is this, that God has given us eternal life, and this life is in His Son. 12 He who has [present active participle] the Son has the life; he who does not have [present active participle] the Son of God does not have the life.

2. Those who are Believing:

John 3:15-16 ...that whoever <u>believes</u> [present, is believing] may in Him have eternal life. 16 "For God so loved the world, that He gave His only begotten Son, that whoever <u>believes</u> [present, is believing] in Him should not perish, but have eternal life.

John 3:36 "The Father loves the Son, and has given all things into His hand. 36 He who <u>believes</u> [present, is believing] in the Son has eternal life; but he who does not obey the Son shall not see life, but the wrath of God abides on him."

John 5:24 "Truly, truly, I say to you, he who hears My word, and <u>believes</u> [present, is believing] Him who sent Me, has eternal life, and does not come into judgment, but has passed out of death into life.

John 6:40 "For this is the will of My Father, that everyone who beholds the Son and <u>believes</u> [present, is believing] in Him, may have eternal life; and I Myself will raise him up on the last day."

John 6:47 "Truly, truly, I say to you, he who <u>believes</u> [present, is believing] has eternal life.

John 11:25-26 Jesus said to her, "I am the resurrection and the life; he who <u>believes</u> [present, is believing] in Me shall live even if he dies, 26 and everyone who lives and <u>believes</u> [present, is believing] in Me shall never die. Do you believe this?"

John 20:31 But these have been written that you may <u>believe</u> that Jesus is the Christ, the Son of God; and that <u>believing</u> [present, is believing] you may have life in His name.

Acts 10:43 ...Of Him all the prophets bear witness that through His name everyone who <u>believes</u> [present, is believing] in Him receives forgiveness of sins."

Rom. 1:16 For I am not ashamed of the gospel, for it is the power of God for salvation to everyone who <u>believes</u> [present, is believing],

Rom. 3:22-24 ...even the righteousness of God through faith in Jesus Christ for all those who <u>believe</u>; [present, are believing] for there is no distinction; 23 for all have sinned [aorist, point action] and fall short [present] of the glory of God, 24 being justified [present present passive indicative] as a gift by His grace through the redemption which is in Christ Jesus;

Rom. 10:4 For Christ is the end of the law for righteousness to everyone who <u>believes</u> [present, is believing].

Rom. 10:10-11 for with the heart man believes [present, is believing], resulting in righteousness, and with the mouth he confesses, resulting in salvation. 11 For the Scripture says, "Whoever believes [present, is believing] in Him will not be disappointed."

1 John 5:13 These things I have written to you who <u>believe</u> [present, are believing] in the name of the

Son of God, in order that you may know that you have eternal life.

3. Those who Believe with Repentance:

Acts 11:18 God has granted to the Gentiles also the repentance {that leads} to life.

Acts 17:30 God is now declaring to men that all everywhere should repent.

Acts 26:20 ...throughout all the region of Judea, and {even} to the Gentiles, that they should repent and turn to God, performing deeds appropriate to repentance.

Acts 26:18 '...to open their eyes so that they may turn from darkness to light and from the dominion of Satan to God, in order that they may receive forgiveness of sins and an inheritance among those who have been sanctified by faith in Me.'

2 Cor. 7:10 For the sorrow that is according to {the will of} God produces a repentance without regret, {leading} to salvation.

4. Those who are Born, and Led by the Spirit:

John 3:3-6 Jesus answered and said to him, "Truly, truly, I say to you, unless one is born again, he cannot see the kingdom of God." ... Jesus answered, "Truly, truly, I say to you, unless one is born of water and the Spirit, he cannot enter into the kingdom of God."

Rom. 8:5-14 For if you are living according to the flesh, you must die; but if by the Spirit you are putting to death the deeds of the body, you will live. For all who are being <u>led by the Spirit of God</u>, these are sons of God.

5. Those who Believe with Obedience and Good Works:

Mat.7:21-23 "Not everyone who says to Me, 'Lord, Lord,' will enter the kingdom of heaven; but <u>he who does</u> [present, is doing] the will of My Father who is in heaven."

John.3:36 "He who believes [present, is believing] in the Son has eternal life; but he who does not <u>obey</u> [present, is not obeying] the Son shall not see life, but the wrath of God abides on him."

John.8:51 "Truly, truly, I say to you, if anyone <u>keeps</u> My word he shall never see death."

John 15:14 "You are My friends, if you <u>do what I command you</u>."

Acts 5:32 And we are witnesses of these things; and {so is} the Holy Spirit, whom God has given to those who <u>obey</u> [present, are obeying] Him.

Rom. 2:6-10,13 Who will render to every man <u>according to his deeds</u>: to those who b<u>y perseverance in doing good</u> seek for glory and honor and immortality, eternal life; but to those who are selfishly ambitious and do not <u>obey</u> the truth, but <u>obey</u> unrighteousness, wrath and indignation. ...but glory and honor and peace <u>to every man who does good</u>, to the Jew first and also to the Greek....for not the hearers of the Law are just before God, <u>but the doers of the Law will be justified</u>.

II Th. 1:8 ...dealing out retribution to those who do not know God and to those who do not <u>obey</u> the gospel of our Lord Jesus.

Heb. 5:9 He became to all those who <u>obey</u> [present, are obeying] Him the source of eternal salvation.

I John 2:4-5 The one who says, "I have come to know Him," and does not <u>keep</u> [present, is not keeping] His commandments, is a liar, and the truth is not in him; but whoever <u>keeps</u> [present, is keeping] His word, in him the love of God has truly been perfected. By this we know that we are in Him.

1 John 2:17 And the world is passing away, and {also} its lusts; but the one who <u>does</u> [present, is doing] <u>the will of God abides forever.</u>

6. Those who are Sanctified—Righteous:

Acts 20:32 And now I commend you to God and to the word of His grace, which is able to build {you} up and to give {you} the inheritance among all those who are <u>sanctified.</u>

Acts 26:18 ...to open their eyes so that they may turn from darkness to light and from the dominion of Satan to God, in order that they may receive forgiveness of sins and an inheritance among those who have been <u>sanctified</u> by faith in Me.

Gal. 5:19-24 Now the deeds of the flesh are evident, which are: ...and things like these, of which I forewarn you just as I have forewarned you that those <u>who practice such things</u> shall not inherit <u>the kingdom of God.</u> ... Now those who belong to Christ Jesus <u>have crucified</u> [aorist active indicative] the flesh with its passions and desires.

Eph. 5:5-6 For this you know with certainty, that no immoral or impure person or covetous man, who is an idolater, has an inheritance <u>in the kingdom of Christ and God.</u> Let no one deceive you with empty words, for because of these things the <u>wrath</u> of God comes upon the sons of disobedience.

Col. 3:3-7 For you <u>have died</u> and your life is hidden with Christ in God. ...Therefore consider the members of your earthly body as <u>dead</u> to immorality, impurity, passion, evil desire, and greed, which amounts to idolatry. For it is on account of these things that the wrath of God will come, and in them you also once walked, when you were living in them.

1Thes 4:7-8 For God has not called us for the purpose of impurity, but in <u>sanctification</u>. Consequently, he who rejects {this} is not rejecting man but the God who gives His Holy Spirit to you.

Heb. 12:14 Pursue peace with all men, and the <u>sanctification without which no one will see the Lord</u>.

I John 3:6-11 No one who abides in Him sins [present, is not sinning]; no one who sins [present, is sinning] has seen Him or knows Him. Little children, let no one deceive you; the one who <u>practices righteousness</u> [present] is righteous, just as He is righteous; the one who practices sin [present] is of the devil; for the devil has sinned from the beginning. The Son of God appeared for this purpose, that He might destroy the works of the devil.

No one who is born of God practices sin [present], because His seed abides in him; and he cannot sin [present, be sinning], because he is born [perfect, was and still is] of God. By this the children of God and the children of the devil are obvious: anyone who does not <u>practice righteousness</u> [present] is not of God.

7. Those who Forgive others:

Mat. 6:12-15 'And forgive us our debts, as we also have forgiven our debtors...' "For if you forgive men for their transgressions, your heavenly Father will also forgive you. But if you do not forgive men, then your Father will not forgive your transgressions."

Mat. 18:32-35 "Then summoning him, his lord said to him, 'You wicked slave, I forgave you all that debt because you entreated me. 'Should you not also have had mercy on your fellow slave, even as I had mercy on you?' "And his lord, moved with anger, handed him over to the torturers until he should repay all that was owed him." So shall My heavenly Father also do to you, if each of you does not forgive his brother from your heart."

8. Those who Separate from the World:

2 Cor. 6:16-18 Or what agreement has the temple of God with idols? For we are the temple of the living God; just as God said, "I will dwell in them and walk among them; and I will be their God, and they shall be My people. "Therefore, come out from their midst and be separate," says the Lord. "And do not touch what is unclean; and I will welcome you. "And I will be a father to you, and you shall be sons and daughters to me," says the Lord Almighty.

Jam. 4:3-4 You adulteresses, do you not know that friendship with the world is hostility toward God? Therefore whoever wishes to be a friend of the world makes himself an enemy of God.

I John 2:15-17 Do not love the world, nor the things in the world. If anyone loves the world, the love of the Father is not in him. For all that is in the world, the lust of the flesh and the lust of the eyes and the boastful pride of life, is not from the Father, but is from the world. And the world is passing away, and {also} its lusts; but the one who does [present, is doing] the will of God abides forever.

9. Those who Surrender to God:

Mark 8:34-37 And He summoned the multitude with His disciples, and said to them, "If anyone wishes to come after Me, let him <u>deny himself</u>, and take up his cross, and follow Me. For whoever wishes to save his life shall lose it; but whoever <u>loses his life</u> for My sake and the gospel's shall save it. For what does it profit a man to gain the whole world, and forfeit his soul? For what shall a man give in exchange for his soul?" (Also Matt.10:38-39; 16:24-25 and Lk.9:23)

Luke 16:13 "No servant can serve two masters; for either he will hate the one, and love the other, or else he will hold to one, and despise the other. <u>You cannot serve God and mammon</u>."

John 12:24-26 "Truly, truly, I say to you, unless a grain of wheat falls into the earth and <u>dies</u>, it remains by itself alone; but if it <u>dies</u>, it bears much fruit. "He who loves his life <u>loses</u> it; and he who <u>hates his life</u> in this world shall keep it to life eternal. "If anyone serves Me, let him follow Me; and where I am, there shall My servant also be; if anyone serves Me, the Father will honor him.

Rom. 6:14-22 For sin shall not be <u>master</u> over you, for you are not under law, but under grace. What then? Shall we sin because we are not under law but under grace? May it never be! Do you not know that when you present yourselves to someone {as} slaves for obedience, you are <u>slaves</u> of the one whom you obey, either of sin resulting in death, or of obedience resulting in righteousness?

But thanks be to God that though you were <u>slaves</u> of sin, you became <u>obedient</u> from the heart to that form of teaching to which you were committed, and having been freed from sin, you <u>became slaves</u> of righteousness. For just as you presented your members {as} <u>slaves</u> to impurity and to lawlessness, resulting in {further} lawlessness, so now present your members {as} <u>slaves to righteousness</u>, resulting in sanctification. For the outcome of those things is death. But now having been freed from sin and <u>enslaved</u> to God you derive your benefit, resulting in sanctification, and the outcome, eternal life.

10. Those who Fear God:

Rom. 11:20-12:1 Quite right, they were broken off for their unbelief, but you stand by your faith. Do not be conceited, but <u>fear</u>; for if God did not spare the natural branches, <u>neither will He spare you</u>. ...

Phil. 2:12 ...presence only, but now much more in my absence, work out [present, be working out] your salvation <u>with fear and trembling</u>;

Heb. 4:1 Therefore, let us <u>fear</u> lest, while a promise remains of entering His rest, any one of you should seem to have come short of it. For indeed we have had good news preached to us, just as they also; but the word they heard did not profit them, because it was not united by faith in those who heard.

1 Pet. 1:17 And if you address as Father the One who impartially judges according to each man's work, conduct yourselves in <u>fear</u> during the time of your stay {upon earth}

Rev. 11:18 ...and {the time} to give their reward to Thy bond-servants the prophets and to the saints and to those who <u>fear</u> Thy name, the small and the great, and to destroy those who destroy the earth.

Rev. 14:7 ... and he said with a loud voice, "<u>Fear</u> God, and give Him glory, because the hour of His judgment has come; and worship Him who made the..."

Rev. 19:5 ...and a voice came from the throne, saying, "Give praise to our God, all you His bond-servants, you who <u>fear</u> Him, the small and the great."

11. Those Who do not Fall Away from the Faith:

Mat.5:13 "You are the salt of the earth; but if the salt has become tasteless, how will it be made salty again? It is <u>good for nothing anymore</u>, except to be thrown out and trampled under foot by men."

Luke 8:13-15 "And those on the rocky {soil are} those who, when they hear, receive the word with joy; and these have no {firm} root; they believe for a while, and in time of temptation <u>fall away</u>. ""And the {seed} which fell among the thorns, these are the ones who have heard, and as they go on their way they are <u>choked with worries and riches and pleasures</u> of {this} life, and bring no fruit to maturity. ... "And the {seed} in the good soil, these are the ones who have heard the word in an honest and good heart, and hold it fast, and bear fruit with ..."

John 15:6 "If anyone does not abide in Me, he is <u>thrown away</u> as a branch, and dries up; and they gather them, and <u>cast them into the fire, and they are burned</u>."

Rom.11:20-23 Quite right, they were <u>broken off for their unbelief</u>, but you stand by your faith. Do not be conceited, but <u>fear</u>; for if God did not spare the natural branches, <u>neither will He spare you</u>. Behold then the kindness and severity of God; to those <u>who fell, severity</u>, but to you, God's kindness, <u>if you continue</u> in His kindness; otherwise you also will be cut off. And they also, <u>if they do not continue</u> in their unbelief, will be grafted in; for God is able to graft them in again.

1 Cor. 10:11-12 Now these things happened to them as an example, and they were written for our instruction, upon whom the ends of the ages have come. Therefore let him who thinks he stands <u>take heed lest he fall</u>.

Gal. 4:9-11 But now that you have come to know God, or rather to be known by God, how is it that you <u>turn back again</u> to the weak and worthless elemental things, to which you desire to be <u>enslaved all over again</u>? You observe days and months and seasons and years<u>. I fear for you</u>, that perhaps I have <u>labored over you in vain</u>.

Gal. 5:4 You have been <u>severed from Christ</u>, you who are seeking to be justified by law; <u>you have fallen from grace</u>.

1 Th. 3:5 I also sent to find out about your faith, for fear that the tempter might have tempted you, <u>and our labor should be in vain.</u>

1 Tm.1:19 ...keeping faith and a good conscience, which <u>some have rejected and suffered shipwreck</u> in regard to their faith.

1 Tm.5:15 ... for some have already turned <u>aside to follow Satan</u>.

1 Tm.4:1 But the Spirit explicitly says that in later times <u>some will fall away from the faith</u>, paying attention to deceitful spirits and doctrines of demons...

1 Tm.4:16 Pay close attention to yourself and to your teaching; <u>persevere in these things; for as you do</u>

this you will insure salvation both for yourself and for those who hear you.

1 Tm. 6:10 For the love of money is a root of all sorts of evil, and some by longing for it have wandered away from the faith, and pierced themselves with many a pang.

1 Tm. 6:21 ...which some have professed and thus gone astray from the faith.

2 Tm.2:12 If we endure, we will also reign with him. If we disown him he will also disown us...

Heb.2:1-3 For this reason we must pay much closer attention to what we have heard, lest we drift away from it... How shall we escape if we neglect so great a salvation?

Heb.3:12 Take care, brethren, lest there should be in any one of you an evil, unbelieving heart, in falling away from the living God.

Heb.4:11 Let us therefore be diligent to enter that rest, lest anyone fall through {following} the same example of disobedience.

Heb.6:5-6 ...and have tasted the good word of God and the powers of the age to come, and {then} have fallen away, it is impossible to renew them again to repentance, since they again crucify to themselves the Son of God, and put Him to open shame.

Heb.10:26-31 For if we go on sinning willfully after receiving the knowledge of the truth, there no longer remains a sacrifice for sins, but a certain terrifying expectation of judgment, and the fury of a fire which will consume the adversaries. Anyone who has set aside the Law of Moses dies without mercy on {the testimony of} two or three witnesses. How much severer punishment do you think he will deserve who has trampled under foot the Son of God, and has regarded as unclean the blood of the covenant by which he was sanctified, and has insulted the Spirit of grace? For we know Him who said, "Vengeance is Mine, I will repay." And again, "The Lord will judge His people." It is a terrifying thing to fall into the hands of the living God.

Heb.12:25 See to it that you do not refuse Him who is speaking. For if those did not escape when they refused him who warned {them} on earth, much less {shall} we {escape} who turn away from Him who {warns} from heaven.

2 Pt.1:10-11 Therefore, brethren, be all the more diligent to make certain about His calling and choosing you; for as long as you practice these things, you will never stumble; for in this way the entrance into the eternal kingdom of our Lord and Savior Jesus Christ will be abundantly supplied to you.

2 Pt.2:20-21 For if after they have escaped the defilements of the world by the knowledge of the Lord and Savior Jesus Christ, they are again entangled in them and are overcome, the last state has become worse for them than the first. For it would be better for them not to have known the way of righteousness, than having known it, to turn away from the holy commandment delivered to them.

Jam. 5:18-20 My brethren, if any among you strays from the truth, and one turns him back, let him know that he who turns a sinner from the error of his way will save his soul from death, and will cover a multitude of sins.

12. Those who Continue to Believe, Remain Faithful, and Endure to the End:

Mat.10:22 "And you will be hated by all on account of My name, but it is the one who has <u>endured to the end who will be saved</u>."

Mat.24:12-13 "And because lawlessness is increased, most people's love will grow cold. But the one <u>who endures to the end, he shall be saved</u>."

Mark12:12 "All men will hate you because of me, but <u>he who stands firm to the end will be saved</u>."

Luke 8:15 "And the {seed} in the good soil, these are the ones who have heard the word in an honest and good heart, and <u>hold it fast, and bear fruit with perseverance</u>.

Luke 9:62 "But Jesus said to him, "No one, after putting his hand to the plow and looking back, is fit for the kingdom of God."

Rom.2:6-8 ...who will render to every man <u>according to his deeds</u>: to those who <u>by perseverance in doing</u> good seek for glory and honor and immortality, <u>eternal life</u>; but to those who are selfishly ambitious and do not obey the truth, but obey unrighteousness, <u>wrath</u> and indignation...

1 Cor.15:2 ...by which also you are saved, <u>if you hold fast the word</u> which I preached to you, unless you <u>believed in vain</u>.

Gal. 6:7-9 Do not be deceived, God is not mocked; for whatever a man sows, this he will also reap. For the one who sows to his own flesh shall from the flesh reap corruption, but the one who sows to the Spirit shall from the Spirit <u>reap eternal life</u>. And let us not lose heart in doing good, for in due time <u>we shall reap if we do not grow weary.</u>

Heb.3:6 ...but Christ was faithful as a Son over His house whose house we are, <u>if we hold fast our</u>

confidence and the boast of our hope firm until the end.

Heb.3:14 We have come to share in Christ if we hold firmly till the end the confidence we had at first.

Heb.6:11-12 And we desire that each one of you show the same diligence so as to realize the full assurance of hope until the end, that you may not be sluggish, but imitators of those who through faith and patience inherit the promises.

Heb.10:23-27 Let us hold fast the confession of our hope without wavering... For if we go on sinning willfully after receiving the knowledge of the truth, there no longer remains a sacrifice for sins, but a certain terrifying expectation of judgment, and the fury of a fire which will consume the adversaries.

Heb.10:35-39 Therefore, do not throw away your confidence, which has a great reward. For you have need of endurance, so that when you have done the will of God, you may receive what was promised. For yet in a very little while, He who is coming will come, and will not delay. But My righteous one shall live by faith; and if he shrinks back, My soul has no pleasure in him. But we are not of those who shrink back to destruction, but of those who have faith to the preserving of the soul.

1 John 2:24 As for you, let that abide in you which you heard from the beginning. If what you heard from the beginning abides in you, you also will abide in the Son and in the Father. And this is the promise which He Himself made to us: eternal life."

Rev.2:7 He who has an ear, let him hear what the Spirit says to the churches. To him who overcomes, I will grant to eat of the tree of life, which is in the Paradise of God.

Rev.2:10-11 Be faithful until death, and I will give you the crown of life. He who has an ear, let him

hear what the Spirit says to the churches. He who
overcomes shall not be hurt by the second death.
Rev.21:7 He who overcomes shall inherit these things,
and I will be his God and he will be My son.

Arrangement by Ken Nissen

"Think About It"

A Reply to "Think About It" questions in *Eternal Security* by Charles Stanley*5

The Rev. Dr. Charles Stanley wrote a book entitled *Eternal Security, Can You Be Sure?* Dr. Stanley writes as though the Scriptures on man's part (obedience, faithfulness) do not count. At the end of each chapter he asks a question regarding man's part/God's part called, "Think About It." We counter his position trying to show what Scripture says. Stanley's questions are given as direct quotes from his book. Scripture is from the NASB and italicized. All emphasis is that of this writer.

Page 10. Stanley: If Christ came to seek and to save that which was lost, and yet we can somehow become unsaved – and therefore undo what Christ came to do – would it not be wise for God to take us on to heaven the moment we are saved in order to insure we make it? Isn't it unnecessarily risky to force us to stay here?

Reply:
  (1) Who are we, the created, to tell the Creator what is wise and best for us? (Rom.9:20, 21).
  (2) God's purpose, His desire, is not to just save us from the penalty of sin, but to save us "from sin" in order

---

5 *Eternal Security, Can You Be Sure?* By Charles Stanley. Thomas Nelson Publishers. 1990.

that we may fellowship with Him –"...*Just as He chose us in Him before the foundation of the world, that we should be holy and blameless*" (Eph.1:4). *For this you know with certainty, that no immoral or impure person or covetous man, who is an idolater, has an inheritance in the kingdom of Christ and God. Let no one deceive you with empty words, for because of these things the wrath of God comes upon the sons of disobedience* (Eph. 5:5-6).

(3) Stanley's conception of the "risk" involved in keeping us here betrays a deep distrust in the power of God to keep us and in the shallowness of our allegiance to God. It's almost as though he's saying God should "kidnap" us and get us to heaven before we change our minds.

(4) In His providence God has many reasons and purposes for us on earth. We know some of them, for instance, to be His instruments to evangelize others.

Page 18. Stanley: If our salvation is not secure, how could Jesus say about those to whom He gives eternal life, **"**a*nd they shall never perish*" (John 10:28)? If even one man or woman receives eternal life and then forfeits it through sin or apostasy, will they not perish? And by doing so, do they not make Jesus' words a lie?

Reply:

Our salvation is secure. It is secure for those who belong to God. One must consider the whole passage and get the context. God said in John 10:26-29, **"***But you do not believe, because you are not of My sheep. "My sheep hear My voice, and I know them, and they follow Me; and I give eternal life to them, and they shall never perish; and no one shall snatch them out of My hand.*" Notice that the secure ones are those who believe, hear with response, unite with Him, and follow Him. These are His sheep, these are secure and these cannot be taken from Him. There is no security for those who are not His sheep.

Page 28. Stanley: Why should God let you into heaven? If your answer includes words such as try my best, church, believe in God, Sunday school, teach, or give, chance are that you still haven't come to grips with the simple truth that salvation is by faith alone. Let me ask the question another way. What are you trusting in to get you into heaven? Is it Christ plus something? Or can you say with confidence that your hope and your trust are in Christ and Christ alone?

Reply:

The statement seems somewhat correct. But why is "believe in God" placed with the "works" items. Stanley seems to say above that "believe in God" for salvation is works yet he says "salvation is by faith alone" — this seems to be conflicting.

Page 40 Stanley: If salvation wasn't permanent, why introduce the concept of adoption? Wouldn't it have been better just to describe salvation in terms of a conditional legal contract between man and God?

Reply:

(1) Stanley's repeated method of deliberately building or implying "straw men" (an exaggerated and false representation of what the other side believes) in order to tear it down and thus, supposedly, prove his view – is not fair nor correct. Salvation is permanent and eternal.

(2) God has adopted those in Christ as His children. But analogies cannot be construed beyond their usage. We have been given a spiritual (not physical) new birth and those in Christ are eternally secure. In John 3 and elsewhere God talks about giving us spiritual life, being re-born spiritually not physically.

Although a son on earth today cannot physically change who his biological father is, he can (and many have) terminated his spiritual union with his earthly father; and/or with his heavenly Father.

Page 59 Stanley: What is the significance of a seal that can be continually removed and reapplied? What does it really seal?

Reply:

(1) "Sealing" here [Eph.1:13], and as it is used in most of the New Testament, means either ownership or truthfulness. Here is a quote from a commentary:

"By giving believers the Spirit, God "seals" or stamps them as his own possession. "...*if anyone has not the Spirit of Christ, he does not belong to him*" (Rom.8:9). Here [Eph.1:13] he is called "*the Holy Spirit of promise.*" ... Probably it indicates that the Holy Spirit brings with him when he is received the promise of glory yet to come." F.F. Bruce, *The New International Commentary on the New Testament.* p.265.

(2) Like a wedding ring the giving of the Spirit demonstrates the union has been joined and an allegiance formed. Like the marriage union it is to be permanent. It would be a serious matter to break such a serious union. It may be impossible to unite, totally reject, and then unite again in such a totally committed relationship.

(3) God nowhere promises protection of a person against himself. God will remain faithful to Himself and His promises, but God will not force a person to remain loyal and united to Him.

Page 66 Stanley: If a man or a woman ends up in hell, who has at some point in life put his or her trust in Christ, doesn't that make what Jesus said to Nicodemus a lie? Or at best only half true?

Reply:

What Jesus said was, "*... that everyone believing into Him should not perish, but have eternal life*" (John 3:16 literal Greek translation). The word "*believing*" when used in the New Testment regarding salvation is <u>consistently</u> used in the Greek present durative tense, and is therefore correctly translated as a current and on-going action. (It is here a present participle active, a believing one.) The one believing in Jesus will not end up in hell. But make no mistake; there is never a promise of eternal life for one who is not believing. Jesus said, "*... but it is the one who has <u>endured to the end</u> <u>who will be saved</u>*" (Matt 10:22).

Page 87 Stanley: If my faith maintains my salvation, I must ask myself, "What must I do to maintain my faith?" For to neglect the cultivation of my faith is to run the risk of weakening or losing my faith and thus my salvation. I have discovered that my faith is maintained and strengthened by activities such as the following: Prayer, Bible Study, Christian Fellowship, Church Attendance, and Evangelism. If these and similar activities are necessary to maintain my faith – and the maintenance of my faith is necessary for salvation – how can I avoid the conclusion that I am saved by my good works?

Reply:

(1) "Faith" is not a password, nor a magical formula, nor a powerful potion that can save someone. Faith is the response to God and the continued union needed that allows us to participate in the benefits of Jesus Christ.

(2) If one agrees that faith is needed for salvation – and that faith on day one of salvation is not works – then to believe the second day is not works either, nor the third day and on and on. If "believing" is "works" then initial believing is also "works" for it is the same faith as it is written, "*As you therefore have received Christ Jesus the Lord, so walk in Him*" (Col 2:6).

(3) "Faith" is trusting and obeying God's Word; which is the opposite of "works" or coming my way.

(4) When we pray, read the Bible, and such; they are a means to strengthen faith, but we do not do so with any reliance on the merit of these activities for salvation. Our salvation comes "via" union with Christ, and is complete with union with Christ, not on what we do for merit: *"He who has the Son has the life; he who does not have the Son of God does not have the life"* (1 John 5:12).

Page 95 Stanley: If our salvation hinges on the consistency of our faith, by what standard are we to judge our consistency? Can we have any doubts at all? How long can we doubt? To what degree can we doubt? Is there a divine quota we dare not exceed?

Reply:

We are saved by union with Christ. We are either joined to Christ or not joined to Him. A husband and wife are either married or not. Husbands and wives do not think in terms of, "How much must I do to remain married?" There is no such thing as union with Christ earned by those who believe to a certain degree or jump certain hurdles. Yet there are responsibilities and allegiance associated with a union, and unions and covenants can be broken when there is rejection of the union by either one.

"...If anyone does not abide in Me, he is thrown away as a branch, and dries up; and they gather them, and cast them into the fire, and they are burned (John 15:1-7). *"For if God did not spare the natural branches, neither will He spare you.... but to you, God's kindness, if you continue in His kindness; otherwise you also will be cut off..."* (Rom 11:20-23).

Page 104 Stanley: If God's holiness compels Him to take back the gift of eternal life from certain believers because of their sin, one of two things is true: Either God compromises His holiness for a time – through their small sins – or man's good works can meet God's requirement for holiness – at least for a short period of time. In that case, Christ died needlessly.

Reply:

(1) The "straw man" here: God does not "take back the gift of eternal life from certain believers because of their sin;" rather certain men may continue in unchecked willful sin which may produce a loss of loyalty to Christ. This is man choosing sin rather than choosing God; not "God taking back."

Paul said to the church, *"Now the deeds of the flesh are... enmities, strife, jealousy, outbursts of anger, disputes, dissensions, factions... and things like these, of which I forewarn you just as I have forewarned you that those who practice such things <u>shall not inherit the kingdom of God</u>"* (Gal 5:19-22).

"Do not be deceived, God is not mocked; for whatever a man sows, this he will also reap. For the one who sows to his own flesh shall from the flesh reap <u>corruption</u>, but the one who sows to the Spirit shall from the Spirit reap <u>eternal life</u>. And let us not lose heart in doing good, for in due time we shall reap if we do not grow weary" (Gal 6:7-10).

(2) Error correction: Eternal life is not a gift as a separate entity from Christ; rather it is one of the many benefits that come to a person who is united to Christ. According to Scripture a man has all spiritual blessings as he is "in Christ" – united with Christ:

"Who has blessed us with every spiritual blessing in the heavenly places in Christ" (Eph 1:3). *"... and the witness is this, that God has given us eternal life, and this life is in His Son* (1 John 5:10-12).

Page 109 Stanley: If God puts a condition on His faithfulness to us, do we not also have a right to put a condition on ours? Can God really expect more of us than He does of Himself?

Reply:

If the motivation behind this question is for God to bend His standards in order to adjust to my life-style and selfish desires, and if "faithfulness" to me is put on that level, then God is not faithful. From another view point, God is always faithful to Himself, to His holy character, and to His promises to us. He has made it abundantly clear that He will not tolerate sin.

His condition is that we repent from sin and turn to Him for salvation. His faithfulness is "conditioned," or based, on being true to His own character and promises. He is always faithful to this. For us it is a matter of our accepting His promises, and trusting His faithfulness to His promises. Who are we to question the wisdom and ways of our good God, or to put a condition on Him?

Page 134 Stanley: If there is an unpardonable sin, Christ did not die for all sin. If He did not die for all sin, there are those to whom salvation is not available to all men, John 3:16 and a multitude of other New Testament verses are not true.

Reply:

It is not that Christ did not die for all sin, but that some have totally and finally said, "No" to Christ. The following is a typical article from Biblical dictionaries and encyclopedias on the "unpardonable sin":

"A sin that is often referred to as the "unpardonable sin" because, in the words of Jesus, "He who blasphemes [speaks evil] against the Holy Spirit never has forgiveness, but is subject to eternal condemnation" (Mark 3:29).

Such slander of the Holy Spirit, Jesus implied, reveals a spiritual blindness, a warping and perversion of the moral nature, that puts one beyond hope of repentance, faith, and forgiveness. Those who call the Holy Spirit Satan reveal a spiritual cancer so advanced that they are beyond any hope of healing and forgiveness." (from *Nelson's Illustrated Bible Dictionary*, Copyright (c)1986, Thomas Nelson Publishers)

Page 138 Stanley: If falling from grace indicates the loss of salvation, why is there no mention of hell? The only threat Paul makes is a return to the "yoke of slavery." As bad as that might be, the threat of hell would certainly carry a great deal more incentive than the possibility of a lifetime of law keeping. Besides, the Jews in Paul's audience were used to living under the law.

Reply:

It is true that "hell" is not referred to in the book of Galatians. What Stanley didn't mention was that the word "hell" is not given in any of Paul's writings. The following are some of the verses from Galatians that indicate the danger of the loss of salvation:

- *I am amazed that you are so quickly deserting Him who called you by the grace of Christ, for a different gospel...should preach to you a gospel contrary to that which we have preached to you, let him be accursed.* (Gal 1:6-9).
- *You foolish Galatians, who has bewitched you, before whose eyes Jesus Christ was publicly portrayed as crucified?... 4 Did you suffer so many things in vain?* (Gal 3:1-4).
- *But now that you have come to know God,... how is it that you turn back again to the weak and worthless elemental things, to which you desire to be enslaved all over again? 10 You observe days and months and*

seasons and years. 11 I fear for you, that perhaps I have labored over you in vain (Gal 4:9-11).

- *My children, with whom I am again in labor until Christ is formed in you* (Gal 4:18-19).

- *I, Paul, say to you that if you receive circumcision, Christ will be of no benefit to you. ... 4 You have been severed from Christ, you who are seeking to be justified by law; you have fallen from grace* (Gal 5:2-4).

- *of which I forewarn you just as I have forewarned you that those who practice such things shall not inherit the kingdom of God* (Gal 5:20-21).

The warnings are real and given in unmistakable terms, and we know that, *"The one having the Son has life; the one not having the Son of God does not have life."* (1 John 5:12 literal translation).

Page 153. Stanley: If Christ was the sacrifice for sin, and yet at the time of his death all your sins were yet to be committed, which of your sins did His blood cover? From the vantage point of the Cross, was there any difference between the sins you committed in the past and those you will commit in the future?

Reply:

It is true that Christ died for all sin and we have full forgiveness of all sin in Christ. Where Stanley is confused is thinking that forgiveness of sin is an entity in itself as a gift of God. What we must understand is that all spiritual blessings from God are ours as we are in Christ. The Gift of God is Jesus: and with Him we have forgiveness, justification, righteousness, adoption, predestination, the Spirit, heaven — we only stand before God as we stand "in Him." Otherwise we have no spiritual blessings – NONE, ZIP, ZERO !!!

Page 159 Stanley: A man does not drift into salvation. Does it really make sense that he can drift out of it? [Heb.2:1-3]

Reply:

Union with Christ is like marriage: people do not drift in and out with marriage/divorce, marriage/divorce on and on because the sacred vows and total allegiance required do not allow for such betrayal. Would it matter how a person turned against Christ (or a spouse)?

It may be by drifting: *"lest we drift away from it"* (Heb 2:1).

By deception: *"You foolish Galatians, who has bewitched you"* (Gal 3:1).

By falling: *"...some will fall away from the faith"* (1 Tim 4:1).

By turning back again: *"...you turn back again ... to be enslaved all over again?* (Gal 4:9).

By unbelief: *"They were broken off for their unbelief, but you stand by your faith. Do not be conceited, but fear; ... for if God did not spare the natural branches, neither will He spare you. ... but to you, God's kindness, if you continue in His kindness; otherwise you also will be cut off..."* (Rom 11:20-23).

By disobedience: *"...fall through following the same example of disobedience"* (Heb 4:11).

In the final analysis we chose to be in a union, and we may choose to leave.

Page 165 Stanley: If Hebrews 6:6 is talking about renewing a person's salvation, doesn't this passage teach that once a person loses salvation, he or she can never regain it? If that is the case, aren't we doing children a great disservice by encouraging them to be born again? Shouldn't we wait until they are much older to lessen the likelihood that they fall away during their teen years and thus lose their salvation forever?

Reply:

Hebrews 6:6 is one of the most difficult passages to understand and there are several plausible interpretations by evangelical scholars. Stanley's interpretation is not among them. Stanley concedes that these are genuine Christian Jews who have "turned their backs on God," "changed their minds and went back to their former religion." Stanley says the lesson this Scripture passage tells us is that "If a Jew...could find salvation through Christ and then walk away from Him without the threat of losing his or her salvation, what do the rest of us have to fear?" p.164-169.

An interpretation of Hebrews 6:6 that is plausible is:
"The writer is saying that when people have entered
into the Christian experience far enough to know
what it is all about and have then turned away,
then, as far as they themselves are concerned, they
are crucifying Christ. In that state they cannot
repent." Leon Morris, *The Expositor's Commentary*
Vol.12. p. 56.

Stanley seems to be saying that we need to manipulate the situation to protect people from the exercise of their own free wills. But God's goal, His desire, is to have people choose Him, believe Him, love Him. He wants those who want Him. Everyone has the free option. Only those who choose Him will be with Him. Yes, those who choose Him must face obstacles to their commitment. God also had to face obstacles in order to win His children. We all are to make the choice: we are to join Him as our Lord and Savior.

Page 174 Stanley: If there is no longer any sacrifice for sins, and the sacrifice for sins took place at Calvary, for which of your sins was sacrifice made?

Reply:

Regarding sacrifice for sin, we must not despise the sacrifice of Christ for that is the only sacrifice that avails to cleanse us and make provision that we be able to stand before the holy God.

Page 181 Stanley: Does it make any sense to say that salvation is offered as a solution for our sin and then to turn around and teach that salvation can be taken away because of our sin?

Reply:

Stanley suggests that some people believe that God "takes away salvation" if they sin. This is certainly false if anyone does believe such. Scripture clearly teaches that God will continue to forgive if we continue to confess our sins (1John 1:9). Men may (and many do) leave God, but God never initiates the leaving, and He will always accept back anyone who truly repents and believes. We reject God and His salvation if we choose another loyalty which undermines our covenant and our loyalty to Christ. God is then no longer our god.

God is always open to anyone who is willing to repent and turn to Him: *"If we confess our sins, He is faithful and righteous to forgive us our sins and to cleanse us from all unrighteousness"* (1 John 1:9). *"For the sorrow that is according to the will of God produces a repentance without regret, leading to salvation"* (2 Cor.7:10). *"...by which also you are saved, if you hold fast the word which I preached to you, unless you believed in vain"* (1 Cor.15:2).

Page 188 Stanley: Can joy and insecurity really coexist? How realistic is it to expect us to rejoice over a relationship that is only as secure as our behavior is consistent?

Reply:

Can a husband and wife have joy in their marriage even though it is possible for either to leave it? Our association with God and His salvation is basically a relationship: *"He who has the Son has life."* God will never be unfaithful nor withdraw His love from us. We can (and multitudes have) withdraw from Him. One who is abiding in Christ has grounds for security; all other grounds are false security. Those who are trusting in a past faith, past decisions, past experiences, yet who are loving the world rather than abiding in Christ have a false security. There are warnings for this:

"You adulteresses, do you not know that friendship with the world is hostility toward God? Therefore whoever wishes to be a friend of the world makes himself an <u>enemy of God</u>" (James 4:4).

"Not everyone who says to Me, 'Lord, Lord,' will <u>enter the kingdom of heaven</u>; but <u>he who does the will of My Father</u> who is in heaven" (Matt 7:21).

Therefore, brethren, be all the more diligent to make certain about His calling and choosing you; <u>for as long as you practice these things</u>, you will never stumble; <u>for in this way the entrance into the eternal kingdom</u> of our Lord and Savior Jesus Christ will be abundantly supplied to you" (2 Peter 1:10,11).

If it Walks Like a Duck

How can I really know that I am a child of God?

"If it looks like a duck, walks like a duck, quacks like a duck, and swims like a duck — it's a duck." This old saying has often been used to say the obvious: something is authentic if it has the authentic characteristics. John said the same thing: *"Whoever claims to live in him must walk as Jesus did"* (1 John 2:6 NIV).

What are the authentic characteristics that show beyond any doubt that one is a child of God? There are numerous references in the New Testament that emphasize the obvious fact that one's life, one's "fruit," shows the authenticity of one's relationship with God, but there is one book that written especially for this, it is the book of First John. John wrote: *"These things I have written to you who believe in the name of the Son of God, in order <u>that you may know</u> that you have eternal life"* (1 John 5:13). How does he say one may know?

LOVE

Many neighborhood bookstore shelves are filled with books on love; magazines are chocked full of love stories; TV programs portray love stories all day long. Everybody loves someone or something even if it is a ball team, a movie, a favorite teapot, or a pet. So how can God say that "love" is a major characteristic of His children? But He does, *"We know that we have passed out of death into life, because we love the brethren. He who does not love abides in death"* (1 John 3:14).

The answer to the dilemma of "love" is that the world and God are talking about two different animals — they are worlds apart — even opposites. The world's idea of love is what is appealing, pleasing, satisfying, or stimulating to oneself. God's love is concerned with the well being of others and how best to serve others — direct opposites. We read that, *"God so loved... he gave his only begotten Son"* (John 3:16). God's children love others even when they don't naturally want to, even when it hurts, even when there is nothing for them in return. The world knows nothing of this love, but it is the primary command and the primary characteristic in God's family.

OBEDIENCE

Sheep follow their shepherd, soldiers obey their captain, players obey their coach, servants obey their master, and children obey their parents. The two most certain proofs of belonging are love and loyalty. John said, *"And by this we know that we have come to know Him, if we keep His commandments. The one who says, "I have come to know Him," and does not keep His commandments, is a liar, and the truth is not in him"* (1 John 2:3-4). Jesus said His sheep hear His voice and follow Him. Obedience shows trust, love, devotion, dedication, praise and loyalty. God's children are those who are obeying Him: *"And having been made perfect, He became to all those who are obeying Him the source of eternal salvation"* (Heb.5: 9). Although as children we do not obey perfectly, obedience is our desire and joy, and we know that He will always give us the grace to obey what He tells us to do.

THE WORLD

God's people love the people of the world, but they must be careful not to become partakers of their selfish/self-serving ways, *"Do not love the world, nor the things in the world. If anyone loves the world, the love of the Father is not in him. For all that is in the world, the lust of the flesh and the lust of the eyes and the boastful pride of life, is not from the Father, but is from the world"* (1 John 2:15-16). God's children are to appreciate and enjoy the good things that God has made for us, but we do not set our primary desires, goals, satisfaction, joy, nor security on these things — only on God Himself.

RIGHTEOUSNESS

Closely related to obedience and love is another major characteristic of a Christian — that of righteousness. The entire Bible is a story of God and His goodness versus the sin and evil in the world. The book of 1 John repeats the theme often portraying God as absolute light, purity, truthfulness, goodness and love. John emphasizes that those in God's family are likewise totally dedicated to this same standard. And although His children are far from His perfection they do manifest a strong resemblance.

A person is saved by joining to Christ, not by trying to be good. However, *"It is written, "You shall be holy, for I am holy"* (1 Peter 1:16). Those who are joined to Christ have entered into His kingdom of righteousness and love; therefore they have accepted this as their way of life. The believers in the various churches were called the "saints." This is the same word as "holy" as in "Holy Spirit" and "God is holy." This is so obvious for God's family that John said those who are not being righteous are not God's children: *"By this the children of God and the children of the devil are obvious: anyone who does not practice righteousness is not of God, nor the one who does not love his brother"* (1 John 3:10).

LIVING TOGETHER

If you ask a husband or wife how they know they are married they will respond that they married, and they are now living together. It's evident. John said that if we are obeying Him we are abiding in Him and He is in us, and we know this from His Spirit abiding in us: *"And the one who keeps His commandments abides in Him, and He in him. And we know by this that He abides in us, by the Spirit whom He has given us"* (1 John 3:24). Jesus said, *"Abide in Me and I in you"* (John 15:4). We live with Jesus; we abide in Him, and He in us by His Spirit.

IN SUMMARY

John puts it simply: Those who are loving God and others, remaining loyal to Him and His ways of righteousness, but not involved in the self centered ways of the world — these are abiding in Him — they have the Son and with Him eternal life: *"And the witness is this, that God gave us eternal life, and this life is in His Son. He who is having the Son is having life; he who is not having the Son of God is not having life"* (1 John 5:11-12 YLT). These children look (spiritually) like Him, act like Him, and live with Him. They are being made more and more into the image of Jesus (Rom.8:29). These may be sure that they are God's children:

"These things I have written to you who believe in the name of the Son of God, in order that you may <u>know</u> that you have eternal life" (1 John 5:13).

"It Is Finished"

Where have you heard, "It is finished?" Yes, Jesus' last words as He hung on the cross. He had just paid the price, the penalty, to redeem us from all our sin. In order to redeem us He had overcome suffering as no other person would ever know. And because He was victorious we can now be joined to Him. Hallelujah. That was the first: *"It is finished."*

But did you know there are two other *"It is finished"* [or *it is done*] in Scripture? One is in Revelation 16:17 when God has had it with the sinful earth and pours out His final wrath called the seventh, the final, Bowl upon earth.

Then the last *"It is finished"* is in the next to last chapter of the Bible, chapter 21. What is this *"It is finished"* all about? What is *"finished"*? The answer: Everything! What the Father and Son had planned from the beginning; what has gone on for the last thousands of years from chapter one of Genesis when God created man, *"in our own image."* From Adam and Eve came the fall, then the flood, Abraham, nation of Israel, the church, all the victories and all the suffering: the whole story of mankind. It is now finished. What is *"finished"*? What has all of history been about? What was worth all the effort, the suffering, the whole process?

We find the answers in chapter 21 verses 1-8.

Verse 1: *"Then I saw a new heaven and a new earth; for the first heaven and the first earth passed away, and there is no longer any sea...."* The old earth and cosmos are gone. A totally new heaven and earth has been created now. Wow! This one is clean and even so much better.

In verse 2 the new city, the new Jerusalem, is the bride: *"And I saw the holy city, new Jerusalem, coming down out of heaven from God, made ready as a bride adorned for her husband"* (Rev.21:2). All judgment is over, the wedding and the wedding feast is past, and the new home is in place. Then there came a loud voice, a shout, from the Father: *"And I heard a loud voice from the throne"* (Rev.21:3). When have you heard the Father speak before? Yes, it was back in the Gospels, on the Mount of Transfiguration, when He said, *"This is My beloved Son, listen to Him."*

Now at the end He speaks again, except this time He shouts because it is now finished. Listen to Revelation 21:3: *And I heard a loud voice from the throne saying, "Now the dwelling of God <u>is with men</u>, and he <u>will live with them</u>. They will <u>be his people</u>, and God himself <u>will be with them</u> and <u>be their God</u>* (NIV).

How many times does the Father say, in this one sentence, that He will be with His children? four or five? Why? You mothers can remember the tough pregnancy days and the labor pains, but when you saw that baby, was it all worth it? Did you not shout, "YEA, YEA"? The Father is now shouting, "YEA, YEA!" He is so happy to be with His children! He is jubilant!

Is He going to take good care of them? Look at the next: *"... and He will wipe away every tear from their eyes; and there will no longer be any death; there will no longer be any mourning, or crying, or pain; the first things have passed away"* (Rev.21:4). None of us mothers and fathers on earth could do all this for our children. Can He fulfill all this?

Look at the next verse, *"And He who sits on the throne said, "Behold, I am making all things new." And He said, "Write, for these words are faithful and true"* (Rev.21:5). Yes, He is able for He is the One who sits on the throne who promises this. He is capable of doing what He promises. And now He has His family all together and complete. Then He said**, *"It is finished!"*** (Rev. 21:6).

This is what it has all been about. The Father, the Son and Spirit were complete in themselves just as a husband and wife are complete in themselves, but children add so much. Now it is a family. Now God has His family and the Son has His beloved. This is God's eternal family in their new home and they are so pleased.

His invitation has been out to all people, and without any charge, it has been completely free. Next He said: *"I am the Alpha and the Omega, the beginning and the end. I will give to the one who thirsts from the spring of the water of life without cost"* (Rev. 21:6). All by His amazing grace from His amazing love.

God has given us the end of the story, the **"It is finished."** This is what He is working toward, and this is what we are to work for and live for. But we are not there yet; not by a long shot. There are many more temptations, trials, hurts, and pain. The war against the world, the flesh and the devil is even escalating. And God is urging each of us to be faithful.

With the next verse God gives His most powerful and important exhortation. It is the key verse of Revelation and perhaps the key verse of the Bible that culminates the main theme: *"He who overcomes will inherit all this, and I will be his God and he will be my son"* (Rev 21:7 NIV).

Wow! To be God's child and beloved of Christ in their eternal home for all eternity. This is the ultimate. He is saying if you want to be with Me and be in my new eternal kingdom, then be my faithful one. It costs nothing and He gives the grace and power by the Spirit that we may be able to choose and to keep choosing Him. The bottom line is "Who wants Me? Who really wants Me? These will be my children."

All down through the ages it has been the same. Many have wanted Him; most have not. Some who wanted Him have paid with their lives. Make no mistake about it, God said it is to those who overcome who will inherit all this and be His dear children.

How can "overcoming" be the factor of all who are part of the eternal family of God? It was the bottom line to each of the seven churches in Revelation chapters 2 and 3. Jesus often said the same: ***"But the one who endures to the end, he shall be saved."*** (Matt 24:13). And Paul said the same:

"Do not be deceived: God cannot be mocked. A man reaps what he sows. 8 The one who sows to please his sinful nature, from that nature will reap destruction; the one who sows to please the Spirit, from the Spirit will reap eternal life. 9 Let us not become weary in doing good, for at the proper time we will reap a harvest if we do not give up" (Gal.6:7-9 NIV).

We are saved by joining to Jesus. This is often called believing in Him or accepting Him as personal Lord and Savior. We are forgiven, born again, and enter His eternal family — at no cost; just by choosing Him. We have then entered a relationship similar to human adoption, marriage, or citizenship.

To later reject the family, live in unfaithful adultery, change our allegiance to another — this is not tolerated by God. There are duties and responsibilities to God just as there are in responsibilities in human relationships. But He gives the grace/power/provision (called grace) to obey and love Him. This remaining faithful to Him is called "overcoming" in Revelation. Those who really want Him respond to His call, and they overcome for Him and by Him. Verse eight tells about those who are not overcomers, but who are the selfish/self-centered rebels.

"But for the cowardly and unbelieving and abominable and murderers and immoral persons and sorcerers and idolaters and all liars, their part will be in the lake that burns with fire and brimstone, which is the second death" (Rev 21:8).

For them the end is fire. Can we imagine what being in hell really means? This is a lake of fire. Everyone has come before God's judgment seat and has been shown a "video" of his life with nothing hidden. Even the thoughts and motives are on display for all to see. All lies, deception, bitterness, jealousy, lust, and covetousness are seen. The only thing each can say is, "I deserve hell." God will say that is what you chose.

So you are thrown screaming into the big black ball or lake. It is so black that you cannot see your hand in front of you. You can cry out, but there is no one to talk to you. You must live with yourself alone. You are very hot. You are thirsty. You are alone and you remember your deeds. You wish you could die but there is no more death. There is no time, no tomorrow, no growing old, no end — it will never get better. There is absolutely no hope and no help — never — no end — no hope. You are in hell. According to God's Word this is what hell is. It is a very serious thing to reject God's offer of His goodness and grace to us. Hell is for those who do not want God; those who reject Him — they will be without Him and all of His benefits.

In Scripture there are incentives for us to choose God:

1. Because to serve the eternal creator God is the right thing to do.
2. Because I want to avoid the eternal punishment in hell.
3. Because I love Him and am grateful to Him for His great salvation in Christ Jesus.
4. Because the creator God knows what is best for me and is my perfect Provider.
5. Because fellowship with Him provides love, joy, and peace.
6. Because He has promised an eternal home for me with Him (and other rewards).
7. Because it will all end the way He has said it will.

These incentives are given in numerous ways throughout Scripture... incentives so that we will overcome for Him and with Him.

The Father so desires the *"It is finished"* that He gave up His Son; and the Son concurred and became identified with man and endured the pain of hell to win His beloved. How great are the incentives for us to join to Jesus! They gave their all that we might be with them. It is His gift with no merit or works of righteousness on our part. No matter how bad we have been Jesus will forgive! WOW!

But joining to the holy God means He is to be Lord. One cannot remain devoted to his selfish/self-centered ways and be joined to Him. This is the way of the world. God said to be part of the sin of the world is being adulterous to Him,

"You adulterous people, don't you know that friendship with the world is hatred toward God? Anyone who chooses to be a friend of the world becomes an enemy of God" (James 4:4-5).

God's way is the opposite; it is God centered; serving Him and others. This is righteousness (See Rom.6). Right now we are still in this selfish/self-centered world, and we are far from perfect, but we can truly desire to please Him. It is when we truly desire to please the other that we are acting in love.

In similar fashion a husband or wife is never perfect to the other. Even when they are not perfect they are still married. And if either later rejects the other in their heart, they have broken the marriage spiritually, even if they are still physically married.

If one loves Jesus he will want to serve and please Him. That one will seek to know what God has said and to obey Him. One's performance may be far from perfection, but his attitude/desire can be right on; it is righteous. God is devoted to us, and He wants us to be devoted to Him. These are the overcomers who will inherit *"all this"* and be His eternal children when **"It is finished."**[6]

---

[6] The "it is finished" in John 19:30 is different word for "finished" from the "it is finished" in Revelation 16 and 21. In John the Greek word "tetelestai" means "to end, to complete, to execute." In Revelation "egeneethee" means "to issue in, to be changed into something, to come to be."

Die to Self?

(A personal testimony)

No, No way! I didn't want to die to self. I knew Jesus died for my sins, and I had "accepted Him as my Lord and Savior." I studied the Bible, went to church, taught Bible lessons, and witnessed for Jesus. I thought I was okay. But I was addicted to sex. It was my pleasure, and I did not want to give it up. In fact, when I tried to give it up, I couldn't.

If I had died back then, would I have gone to heaven? According to Paul the answer is, "No.":

> *"The acts of the sinful nature are obvious: sexual immorality, impurity and debauchery; idolatry and witchcraft; hatred, discord, jealousy, fits of rage, selfish ambition, dissensions, factions, envy; drunkenness, orgies, and the like. I warn you, as I did before, that those who live like this* **will not inherit the kingdom of God**. *... Those who belong to Christ Jesus have crucified the sinful nature with its passions and desires"* (Gal 5:19-24 NIV).

Jesus said I would have to die to self,

> *"If anyone would come after me, he must deny himself and take up his cross and follow me. For whoever wants to save his life will lose it, but whoever loses his life for me and for the gospel will save it. 36*

What good is it for a man to gain the whole world, yet forfeit his soul?" (Mark 8:34-38 NIV).

Therefore according to the Bible I had a false sense of security for many years. I was living in sin so Jesus was not really my Lord and Savior.

On June 2, 1986 I came to my senses (by His grace). I saw how sinful and futile my life had been. I asked if He would forgive me and have me? He said so clearly, "That is why I reached out my arms." I said, "I am yours now and forever." He said, "I am yours." WOW! What a time. I always remember it with tears.

But it was not until then that I realized I had never died to self. He was not really my Lord before. If He had been "Lord" I would have done what He wanted, not my pleasure.

But how to get the power to change and do what He wants? It was not easy. I had habitually been thinking in the wrong way all my life. I had to learn to immediately reject those thoughts and to think only what would please Him. He has promised to always give the grace (provision) to obey Him, and He does. He gives the grace for whatever we need — when we need it. We are never strong, but with His Spirit in us we have the power of the universe — even enough power for this sinful man.

There are always temptations from the world, the flesh, and the devil, but now the choice has already been made — "whatever you want, my Lord." I am never perfect, but my attitude and desires are on the mark. My life is now full of love, joy and peace without more regrets. I have many regrets about my past, but He has forgiven me, and now I am His and He is mine — forever. Die to self? OH YES!!!

The Creator stretched out His arms because He wanted me/us to be with Him in His family — even for the likes of me. I am so grateful! I am so thankful! Now I think of others who are not united with Him. Oh how they need Him.

Some Bible Verses on Death to Self

Matt 16:24-26 *Then Jesus said to his disciples, "If anyone would come after me, he must deny himself and take up his cross and follow me. 25 For whoever wants to save his life will lose it, but whoever loses his life for me will find it. 26 What good will it be for a man if he gains the whole world, yet forfeits his soul?* (NIV)

Rom 6:1 *What shall we say, then? Shall we go on sinning so that grace may increase? 2 By no means! We died to sin; how can we live in it any longer? 3 Or don't you know that all of us who were baptized into Christ Jesus were baptized into his death? ... 5 If we have been united with him like this in his death, we will certainly also be united with him in his resurrection. 6 For we know that our old self was crucified with him so that the body of sin might be done away with, that we should no longer be slaves to sin... 7 because anyone who has died has been freed from sin.* (NIV)

Rom 8:9-14 *And if anyone does not have the Spirit of Christ, he does not belong to Christ. 10 But if Christ is in you, your body is dead because of sin, yet your spirit is alive because of righteousness. ... 13 For if you live according to the sinful nature, you will die; but if by the Spirit you put to death the misdeeds of the body, you will live, 14 because those who are led by the Spirit of God are sons of God.* (NIV)

2 Tim 2:11-12 *If we died with him, we will also live with him; 12 if we endure, we will also reign with him.* (NIV)

Col 3:1-6 *Since, then, you have been raised with Christ, set your hearts on things above, where Christ is seated at the right hand of God. ...3 For you died, and your life is now hidden with Christ in God... 5*

Put to death, therefore, whatever belongs to your earthly nature: sexual immorality, impurity, lust, evil desires and greed, which is idolatry. 6 Because of these, the wrath of God is coming. (NIV)

Gal 5:24 *Those who belong to Christ Jesus have crucified the sinful nature with its passions and desires.* (NIV)

Trust & Obey

Acknowledgments:

Thank you my dear wife, Margaret, for allowing me the time needed to concentrate and to write while I worked on these books. I love you.

Many thanks to my dear friend, counselor, Bible scholar, and former pastor, Vernon L. Bauer, for all he has helped me with through the last twenty something years; and for his help in editing this book.

Whenever I needed help with my multiple technical and computer problems I called our grandson, C.J. Owensby. He is so smart (intelligent), knowledgeable, and willing to help. Thank you, CJ.

Our home church body has been so loving and helpful over the years. Thank you our dear friends, our brothers and sisters in Christ.